157/61

4/6

GOOD COMPANY IN
OLD WESTMINSTER
AND THE TEMPLE

"LITTLE ANNE" RICKMAN
Afterwards Mrs. Lefroy

GOOD COMPANY

IN OLD WESTMINSTER
AND THE TEMPLE

BY

CONSTANCE HILL

FOUNDED ON THE EARLY RECOLLEC-
TIONS OF ANNE (RICKMAN) LEFROY

ILLUSTRATED BY REPRODUCTIONS
FROM CONTEMPORARY SKETCHES
PRINTS AND PORTRAITS

JOHN LANE THE BODLEY HEAD LTD.

First Published in 1925

MADE AND PRINTED IN GREAT BRITAIN BY
WILLIAM CLOWES AND SONS, LIMITED, LONDON AND BECCLES

PREFACE

THIS book, as its title indicates, leads us into the interesting society of long ago formed by men who have left their indelible mark upon English literature. Here we meet them in their everyday life and seem as it were to converse with them on equal terms. We feel the potent charm of Charles Lamb and the sweet influence of his sister Mary; we imagine we can hear for the moment the eloquent words of Coleridge and of Hazlitt.

The friends met for Lamb's Wednesday evening gatherings, sometimes in his own rooms on an upper storey of 4, Inner Temple Lane, sometimes in the house of Admiral Burney, and sometimes in the house of John Rickman and his wife in the Speaker's Court Yard of Westminster ; John Rickman being Secretary to the Speaker, as is well known from his *Life*, so ably written by Orlo Williams, which was published in 1911.

It is to their daughter, " Little Anne," who in later years became Mrs. Lefroy, that we owe the Early Recollections of their life in Old Westminster. She it is who supplies the child-element in this volume so acceptable amidst the sayings and doings of grown-up people.

The *Early Recollections* were originally recorded for the pleasure of Mrs. Lefroy's nieces, the Misses Hone, who have most kindly given me leave to make use of them in this book, and for which I should like to express my gratitude here.

Orlo Williams made occasional use of portions of the *Early Recollections* in his *Life of John Rickman*.

I am much indebted to my friend, Miss Grace Lefroy, for her kind and ready help in lending me her mother's interesting sketches of bits of Old Westminster for reproduction, also for the loan of a silhouette portrait of " Little Anne," and in other ways.

By the courtesy of the Editor of the *Architect's Journal* I am able to reproduce a print of the doorway of Shelley's house in Great College Street, long since demolished.

The writing of this book has been a source of much happiness to me, and it is an effort to bring it to a close and to turn away from those whom I have learnt to love.

I may perhaps entertain a hope that their ennobling influence may be felt by some of my readers as well as by myself—unless indeed it is a pleasure they already enjoy.

CONSTANCE HILL.

GROVE COTTAGE,
FROGNAL,
HAMPSTEAD.

CONTENTS

LIST OF ILLUSTRATIONS

ix

GOOD COMPANY IN OLD WESTMINSTER AND THE TEMPLE

Southey, a valued friend of Rickman's, wrote to him on this child's birth in a humorous vein : " Your good news came much sooner than it was expected. I shall not condole with you on the daughtership, because (though it would be an error deserving of flogging to deny that the masculine gender is more worthy than the feminine) there are many things in which girls are preferable to boys. They begin to be useful just when boys begin to be troublesome ; you have them longer for companions, and moreover the cost of a boy's education is a girl's fortune.   Mrs. Rickman, I daresay, is well satisfied with the sex— or if she is not she will soon find cause to be so. Boys about a house are like favourite dogs in the country who come into the parlour with dirty legs and then lie down on the hearth and lick themselves clean ; they are always in the way, and when out of sight, ten to one but they are in mischief. Girls are like cats, clean and fit to be upstairs." *

" Little Anne " in after years as Mrs. Lefroy recorded her early Recollections of her life in Westminster for the benefit of her nieces the Miss Hones, by whose kindness I am allowed to use them for this volume.

" What I remember almost first of all in my young days," she writes, " was when we lived in the old house in New Palace Yard which was the official

* See *Life of Robert Southey*, by John Dennis.

THE SPEAKER'S COURTYARD

A lantern over the Rickman's door

residence of the Speaker's Secretary. Our house was in a small court entered by two archways, the Speaker's Archway, we called one . . . our front door was in an old stone wall opposite the Westminster Hall wall . . . close to our door was a narrow door and passage which led into a garden in which were Laburnum trees and a lawn. This was Mr. Wilde's garden. The passage passed under some official rooms of the Exchequer—an old wooden building of Queen Elizabeth's time standing on wooden legs. Mr. Wilde held the Office of Keeper of the Exchequer, and when the clerks were gone from their duties, the keys were carried to his house ; this stood so close to the river Thames that at Spring tide there was great pleasure to us children in dipping our fingers down into the water from the sitting-room windows."

From what Mrs. Lefroy writes of the situation of their house, it is evident that it was very near to one side of Westminster Hall. In a contemporary print of the Hall after a picture by Thomas Sanby which we give, it will be seen how different its surroundings were in Mrs. Lefroy's day to what they are now. The wide open space in front of the Hall was then paved with cobble stones and there were low irregular houses on either side. On the river side of the Hall, where the imposing terrace is now to be seen, was a collection of red-roofed houses of various shapes and sizes which rose from the edge of the water.

Writing of Mr. Wilde's house and family, Mrs. Lefroy remarks : " How well I remember that house and those dear friends who loved me and petted me as though I were their little niece, and beckoned me to run to them when I was standing half expecting their beckon, on one of Papa's Official Oak boxes in his Book room window ! How much better our house was than Mr. Wilde's, because it was at the beginning of the garden, so we had a bright pleasant piece of ground with a terrace and rails to the river. The roses and other flowers grew very luxuriantly, and against the end of Mr. Wilde's house on the terrace there was a Hamboro' grape ; and we had gooseberries too and a Morella cherry. . . . Papa very often, in warm weather, stretched himself down on the slope of turf that formed the Terrace. He generally went to sleep and we made Daisy chains to dress him up, and looked at his pigtail, but we never quite made up our minds to pull it."

We would pause here in order to make the reader acquainted with the family of " little Anne." It consisted of Mr. and Mrs. John Rickman, their two daughters Anne and Frances and their son William. Frances had been so named after Madame d'Arblay (Fanny Burney), with whose brother, Admiral James Burney, they were on terms of friendship. In the Life of John Rickman, so ably written by Orlo Williams, we learn of the great respect and even of affection in which he was held by many of the prominent men of literature of the day, some of whom we shall meet in these pages.

It was early in the century that Rickman first made the acquaintance of Charles Lamb—an acquaintance which soon ripened into friendship. " He is a most pleasant hand," writes Lamb to a friend, " a fine rattling fellow, who has gone through life laughing at solemn apes ; himself hugely literate, from matter of fact to Xenophon and Plato ; he can talk Greek with Porson, and nonsense with me . . . fullest of matter with least verbosity." And later on, when Rickman went to Ireland for a time, Lamb wrote : " I have lost by his going what seems to me I can never recover—a *finished man.* . . . His memory will come to me as the brazen serpent to the Israelites."

Coleridge called him a sterling man and assured him of his unaffected esteem, and Southey wrote to him, " God bless you, my dear R. I would often give much for a quiet evening's conversation with you."

Those who knew Rickman intimately recognized the gentler side of his character, but by the outer world he was regarded as a somewhat stern and rigid man of business. Although numbering so many poets

as his friends, he wrote to Southey on one occasion :
" Poetry has its use and its place and like some known
superfluities we should feel awkward without it (but)
I think poetry bad in a man who may be better
employed ; a toy in manhood."

The style of living in the Rickman household was
simple, and it was carried on upon lines laid down
by the Master of the House. He disliked dinner
parties as causing undue expense and also, as he says,
" leading to half a dozen unnecessary glasses of wine,
and which separate the sexes very ridiculously during
the best hours of the evening." The usual dinner-
hour of the Rickmans was four o'clock, but friends
often gathered at their house at the tea hour.

We are told that the living rooms were on the first
floor, the largest of them having three windows
looking on to the river. It was called the sitting-room.
Here it was that the family lived entirely when alone,
but when guests were with them a second parlour
called the " Book room " was used for meals.

Mrs. Lefroy describes her father's attire for
ordinary occasions and also for official ceremonies.
" For ordinary occasions he wore," she says, " tight-
woven woollen Oxford mixture pantaloons and grey
socks, and very pointed toes to his shoes ; his shirt
frill was very neatly plaited and his cravat of fine
white nainsook was tied in a bow. His coat was cut
like an evening coat is now. Every day at four

OLD WESTMINSTER FROM THE RIVER

From a sketch by Anne Rickman, afterwards Mrs. Lefroy

o'clock Papa went with the Speaker in full dress to
the House of Commons ; then he wore black silk
stockings to the knee and steel buckles, (also) a very
sparkling steel-handled sword at his side. He had
(usually) frills and cuffs of lace but when in mourning
(they were) of muslin. The hair-dresser came every
day and curled and powdered his hair, ' just before
breakfast.' "

Rickman was not fond of finery and he found
the perpetual dressing in such an elaborate style
very irksome ; but he devised a partial remedy.
" I begin to become less irritated with the daily
nonsense of Bag and Sword," he writes to a friend,
" and have reduced the ceremony of dressing in
costume to 7 minutes—undressing 2 minutes—I
have a wig to which the bag is appended."

One of " little Anne's " earliest recollections is
in connection with the great frost of 1813–14, when
the Thames was frozen over. " When I stood on
the box in the Bookroom window," she writes, " I
saw the tent floating down with the tide on the ice,
and a roast ox was prepared on it for the wonder of
the thing. This island of ice went up and down,
I think, for several days."

Again she writes : " I can just remember going to
stand in the long lobby of the Speaker's house with
Mr. Ley's two little girls to see a party of grandees
pass by to luncheon in the House of Commons Dining

Room. It was Queen Charlotte and the Duke and Duchess of Wellington after the Battle of Waterloo. I remember Queen Charlotte had powdered hair and the Duchess had a white bonnet and was stouter than the Queen. It must have been the day when the Duke came to the House of Commons to receive Public Thanks and the Speaker Abbott made him a speech."

The dining-room alluded to, she tells us, had a groined ceiling and was formerly the Crypt of St. Stephen's Chapel.

Again she writes : " By way of recording the costume of those days say 1818 I will introduce you to the pavement before Westminster Hall on Sunday morning, when the last bell of the Church was calling us to service, first The Speaker and his wife—Mr. and Mrs. Abbott, her bright emerald silk pelisse, trimmed with deep ermine, a muff as large as a pillow, deep cuffs and a long tippet, the footman behind with her Prayer Book ; Mr. Abbott with Pig-tail and broad-brimmed hat, a black swallow-tailed coat, tight grey Pantaloons and Hessian boots, rather short with a tassel in front. My father much the same dress also with a Pig-tail. Mamma had Sable en suite, her Pelisse was ' Waterloo blue ' silk, the Sable at the bottom 6 or 8 inches wide. The muff very large indeed . . . then came Mr. and Mrs. Dyson and their little daughter Marianne, he in country gentleman's costume, the Pig-tail, white stockings with short nankeen gaiters, and the short knee breeches of light drab or nankeen, a striped linen waistcoat, white cravat and a coat of snuff-brown cloth. Then Mr. and Mrs. Wilde, she in black and black lace (swansdown muff) with long tippet of the same ; he with black silk stockings and shorts buckled to his knees, high shoes, tied in good bows, a large silver-headed stick, powdered hair and a very large important Pig-tail under his large hat. Marianne Dyson, I remember, had little gaiters of nankeen over her white stockings and a nicely plaited frill to her little white round tippet.

" In winter, I think, beaver bonnets, light drab with feathers to match were universal."

CHAPTER II

THE LAMBS AND THE BURNEYS

WE have already spoken of the friendship existing between the Rickmans and the Burneys, and it is pleasant to meet with members of these families from time to time in the pages of the *Recollections*.

Admiral James Burney (Fanny Burney's elder brother) had married a Miss Sally Payne, daughter of Mr. Thomas Payne, the celebrated bookseller, whose small old-fashioned shop (a mere " elbow shed " lighted by a skylight) was situated at the Gate of the lower " Mewes " near Leicester Square. Here it was that the leading men of letters of the latter half of the eighteenth century constantly resorted for pleasant and easy chat, and when a fine new bookshop was opened by a rival near at hand with a view to drawing off some of these famous loungers, the force of habit proved too strong for them and they remained faithful to the small, dark, encumbered shop.

At the time we are writing of, the business had

passed into the hands of a son of Mr. Payne's and his partner Mr. Foss who had quitted the Mewes Gate and established themselves in Pall Mall. Their shop also became celebrated. Mrs. Lefroy in the *Recollections* speaks of " Mr. Payne's library of rare volumes folio and others," and says " in those days Noblemen thought much of such and gave fabulous prices for a rare and only copy. I remember," she adds, " the grand room of books. It was of Mr. Payne that our rare and valuable copy of the illustrated Gough's *Camden's Britannia* was purchased by our Father, the price (being) 113 guineas."

Fanny Burney, writing of Miss Payne and her sister in 1775, says : " The eldest is very pretty and about 18 years of age ; she is modest, gentle and obliging. The younger has, I believe, a deeper understanding but is neither so handsome nor so pleasing as her sister." We presume that Sally was the prettier Miss Payne, as she is described as very good looking in later life and her young daughter was named Sally. Her marriage with Captain Burney, R.N., took place in 1786.

At the period of which we are writing Admiral and Mrs. Burney were living at No. 26, James Street, Westminster. He had retained his character for oddity and good humour so often mentioned in Fanny Burney's Diaries. We read in the *Recollections* : " In those days there was Sally Burney. Our Father was very kind to her, for ' the old captain ' R.N. her Father was an ' odd fish ' and her wardrobe therefore very scanty though her mother's good taste would have wished it otherwise. I remember the dark blue velvet ' Spencer ' that he gave her.

" Her Father was always occupied in his small parlour at a green baize table writing his Folio History of the South Sea Islands. He went round the world with Captain Cook ; and Colonel Phillips (of the Marines), who did the same, was also with Captain Cook when he was murdered at Otaheite and carried him on his back through the water."

This is not quite correct—it was impossible to bring away the body of Captain Cook, but Phillips jumped into the water to save a drowning companion and in spite of the weapons hurled after them by the savages he managed to bring his friend safe into their ship. Captain Phillips afterwards married James Burney's sister Susan, a singularly interesting woman, but at the period of the *Recollections* he had become a widower. His title was now that of Colonel.

" This Colonel Phillips," writes Mrs. Lefroy, " I remember very well. He was always very good-natured to me—gave me curiosities, the fruits of his constant visits to the British Museum where I fancy he was ever to be seen lounging and offering advice, or a hand when any novelty arrived. ' The small

Memnon ' was, I know, very much in his mind and small fragments of its reddish granite he gave to me. He had a turning machine and made small vases after the antique, using perhaps a dozen kinds of wood, relics of his distant voyages. The old gentleman was quite of the old school of heavy make with a scissoim always between waistcoat and trousers and a large bald head, very spare of hair." In a letter to Southey, Charles Lamb, when giving a list of his particular friends, mentions " the high-minded associate of Cook, the veteran Colonel (Phillips), with his lusty heart still sending cartels of defiance to old Time."

Both Admiral Burney and Colonel Phillips were regular attendants at the whist parties held sometimes in the Rickmans' house, sometimes in Admiral Burney's house in Westminster, though more often in the house of Charles and Mary Lamb in the Temple at their celebrated Wednesday and afterwards Thursday evenings.

In an early memoir of Lamb written by Mr. Forster we read : " Mr. Lamb's earliest associates in London were Wordsworth, Coleridge, Southey, Charles Lloyd, and others who called Admiral Burney friend." They used to assemble weekly at the Burneys' house at the Queen's Gate to chat and play whist ; or they would meet to discuss supper, and the hopes of the world, at the Old Salutation and

Cat, a little public house in the neighbourhood of Smithfield, " where they would remain long after they had heard the chimes at midnight."

Mrs. Lefroy tells us in her *Recollections* that " Charles Lamb and his sister often came upon the scene, he so very black, thread lace stock, quite as ' Elia ' should be, rather the air of a Dissenting Minister, underhung and making a pun in a low voice in a distant corner of the room where he generally seated himself, his good sister Mary Lamb, a stout roundabout little body with a Turban and a layer of snuff on her upper lip. She was so goodnatured, and had a gruff kind of voice. I liked her very much and read over and over again her charming story-book entitled *Mrs. Leicester's School.*"

There was a marked likeness between Charles and Mary Lamb it seems. The features of both were regular, their eyes dark and expressive and " their smile winning in the extreme." Mary was below the middle height in stature, and Charles tells us incidentally in one of his Essays, that his height was only five feet four inches. Mary had a slight hesitation in her speech which resembled in a softened degree her brother's stammer. " That pleasant little stammer," as Barry Cornwall styles it, " just enough to prevent his making speeches, just enough to make you listen eagerly for his words."

A tender tie of affection existed between the

CHARLES LAMB *(ELIA)*
By Maclise

brother and sister. When they were in company together Mary's eyes would follow him everywhere, we are told, and even when he was standing at the other end of the room she would supply some word that he wanted.

Mary was much loved by the more intimate friends of her brother and valued for her ready sympathy and powers of consolation in times of trouble. Leigh Hunt in one of his writings thus apostrophizes her : " And thou M. L. why have I not the art, like the old writers of dedications, of at once loading thee with panegyric and saving the shoulders of thy modesty ? "

Mrs. Lefroy tells us that " Mrs. Burney was constant at the Whist table which was the usual amusement at these evening meetings. (Admiral) Burney's *Book on Whist* was a great authority. The Whist Purse was one of the elegant additions to the Toilette, often of beads or gold thread. Let me add that there was no spirit of gambling at all but the genius of the game enjoyed."

Of the many contemporary writers who have described the whist parties of the pleasant clique are Talfourd and Leigh Hunt. The latter writes : " Talk not to me of great houses in which such things (as card playing) occur, for there the whist players are gamblers and the non-whist players are nobody at all. Here the whist was for its own sake and yet the non-players were tolerated."

One of the most regular players was Admiral Burney, " the frank-hearted voyager with Captain Cook round the world," as Talfourd calls him, " who seemed to unite our society with the circle over which Dr. Johnson reigned."

We read in Fanny Burney's *Diary* that the Doctor took a lively interest in young " Jim Burney," and on his being appointed to the command of his first ship in 1781, Doctor Johnson wrote to Mrs. Thrale : " I delight to hear of the happiness diffused among the Burneys. I question if any ship upon the ocean goes out attended with more good wishes than that which carries the fate of Burney."

Talfourd tells us that Admiral Burney " used to talk of his schooldays under the tutelage of Eugene Aram ; how he remembered the gentle usher pacing the playground arm-in-arm with someone of the elder boys ; and seeking relief from the unsuspected burthen of his conscience by talking of strange murders, and how he, a child, had shuddered at the handcuffs on his teacher's hands when taken away in the postchaise to prison."

It seems that Mrs. Burney, who was so constant at the whist table, is the original of Mrs. Battle in Elia's Essay entitled " Mrs. Battle's Opinions on Whist."   There is a difference, however, between them as regards age, for Mrs. Burney was a younger woman than Mrs. Battle.

"A clear fire, a clean hearth and the rigour of the game. This was the celebrated *wish* of old Sarah Battle," writes Elia. "She loved a thorough-paced partner and a determined enemy. She took and gave no concessions. She hated favours. . . . She fought a good fight ; cut and thrust. She held not her good sword (her cards) like a dancer. She sat bolt upright, and neither showed you her cards nor desired to see yours.

" . . . I never in my life—and I knew Sarah Battle many of the best years of it—saw her take out her snuff-box when it was her turn to play ; or snuff a candle in the middle of the game ; or ring for a servant till it was fairly over." And alluding to triflers who attach no seriousness to the game Elia remarks : "Of such it may be said that they do not play at cards but only play at playing them. . . . Sarah Battle was none of that breed."

But in spite of her devotion to the "rigour of the game " Mrs. Burney, who had a kind and gentle heart, would make use of a pause occurring, when "little Anne " happened to be present, to send out to a neighbouring pastrycook's shop for a jam tart, much to that small person's satisfaction.

Talfourd has left us excellent descriptions of Charles Lamb's Wednesday (afterwards Thursday) evening gatherings when he and his sister were living in the Temple.

C

" Now turn to No. 4 Inner Temple Lane at ten o'clock," he writes, " when the sedater part of the company are assembled and the happier stragglers are dropping in from the play. Let it be any autumn or winter month when the fire is blazing steadily and the clean swept hearth and Whist tables speak of the spirit of Mrs. Battle, and serious looks require the ' rigour of the game.' The furniture is old-fashioned and worn ; the ceiling low and not wholly unstained by traces of the ' great plant ' though now virtuously forborne ; but the Hogarths, in narrow black frames, abounding in infinite thought, humour and pathos, enrich the walls ; and all things wear an air of comfort and hearty English welcome.

" Lamb himself, yet unrelaxed by the glass, is sitting with a sort of Quaker primness at the whist-table, the gentleness of his melancholy smile half lost in his intentness on the game ; his partner (Godwin) . . . is regarding his hand with a philosophic but not a careless eye. Captain Burney only not venerable because so young in spirit sits between them and H. C. R. (Henry Crabb Robinson) who alone now and then breaks the proper silence to welcome some incoming guest, is his happy partner—true winner in the game of life whose leisure achieved early, is devoted to his friends. . . . In one corner of the room you may see the pale earnest countenance of Charles Lloyd who is discoursing ' of fate, free-will and foreknowledge absolute' with Leigh Hunt and with Basil Montagu, gentle enthusiast in the cause of humanity who is pouring into the outstretched ear of George Dyer some tale of legalized injustice which the recipient is vainly trying to comprehend."

Among the whist players Talfourd mentions " Rickman, the sturdiest of jovial companions, severe in the discipline of Whist as at the table of the House of Commons of which he was the principal clerk."

" Soon the room begins to fill ; in slouches Hazlitt from the theatre where his stubborn anger for Napoleon's defeat at Waterloo has been softened by Miss Stephens's angelic notes which might ' chase anger, and grief, and fear and sorrow, and pain from mortal or immortal minds.' Kenney (the dramatist) with a tremulous pleasure, announces that there is a crowded house to the ninth representation of his new comedy, of which Lamb lays down his cards to inquire ; or Ayrton,* mildly radiant, whispers the continued triumph of Don Giovanni for which Lamb, incapable of opera, is happy to take his word. Now and then an actor glances in as from ' the rich Cathay ' of the world behind the scenes, with news of its brighter human-kind, and with looks reflecting the public favour—Liston grave beneath the weight of the town's regards—or Miss Kelly, unexhausted in spirit by alternating the drolleries of high farce

* Director of the music at the Italian Opera.

with the terrible pathos of melodrama—or Charles
Kemble mirrors the chivalry of thought, and ennobles
the party by bending on them looks beaming with the
aristocracy of nature.

" Meanwhile Becky lays the cloth on the side
table under the direction of the most quiet, sensible
and kind of women who soon compels the younger
and more hungry of the guests to partake largely
of the cold roast lamb or boiled beef, the heaps of
smoking roast potatoes and the vast jug of porter
. . . the various driblets of talk combine into a stream,
while Miss Lamb moves gently about to see that
each modest stranger is duly served ; turning now
and then an anxious loving eye on Charles."

Barry Cornwall, describing these Wednesday
evenings, writes : " Politics (especially party politics)
were seldom admitted. Lamb disliked them as a theme
for evening talk . . . and when Hazlitt's impetuosity
drove him, as it sometimes did, into fierce expressions
on public affairs, these were usually received in silence,
and the matter thus raised up for assent or controversy
was allowed to drop. The beauty of these evenings
was that every one was placed upon an easy level.
No one out-topped the others. No one—not even
Coleridge—was permitted to out-talk the rest. No
one was allowed to hector the others, or to bring his
own grievances too prominently forward so as to
disturb the harmony of the night." The writer

goes on to say, " I never in all my life heard such unpretending good sense talked as at Lamb's social parties. Often a piece of sparkling humour was shot out that illuminated the whole evening. Sometimes there was a flight of high and earnest talk, that took one half-way towards the stars."

CHAPTER III

" LITTLE ANNE "

RICKMAN, we are told, was a somewhat stern although an affectionate father. His views on education were peculiar. When Anne's younger sister Frances was sent to a school in Brighton for the benefit of her health it was supposed by Anne's well-wishers that a governess would be engaged to assist in her education, but that was not done. " Papa looked down," writes Mrs. Lefroy, " upon any routine of teaching and discipline. He considered no one should be pressed to learn. ' There were plenty of books,' he would remark (folios), ' on the shelves for Miss Anne to read if she cared to do so.' In truth," she writes, " I did not care and I am very sorry that I had no stiff training. I generally was occupied seated square before a sheet of ' Pot Paper ' copying out some Official papers, circulars or otherwise, or drawing papers from beneath Papa's hand just so exactly that he could go on signing paper after paper without any pause to the number of 500 perhaps !   Now you see," she adds, " why I never could stitch, but always could write."

There was no end to the official papers, for Rickman held the post of Secretary to the Board of Public Works, whose documents were kept in large oaken boxes in the " Book Room." " Those boxes ! " exclaims Mrs. Lefroy, " what old memories arise as I have them before me now in my mind's eye !   One had ' Highland Roads and Bridges ' printed in large letters on its top.   How many hundred times did I write those words when my writing had become worthy to be used for the sheet notices issued to the Commissioners for meetings !   Mr. Abbott was active and fond of stirring and promoting work ; the meetings took place at his official residence (the Speaker's House) next door.   He had in his Secretary a man after his own heart, ever hungry for work, powerful in mind and body."

We are told by a daughter of Mrs. Lefroy that " after the purchase of Gough's *Camden's Brittania* ' Little Anne ' was employed by her Father, though not more than 12 years old when she began it, to make an Index of all the prints (over 700 in number) in the 31 Folio volumes.   She was seated at a special table made for the occasion.   The Index, which was divided into counties, was afterwards bound in red leather."

" Little Anne " had early shown taste for drawing,

and her father arranged for her to have lessons in water-colour painting from a Miss Atkinson. She was encouraged to sketch from Nature and was able in time to portray some of the bits of Old Westminster with its pretty rural gardens that have long since disappeared and which we are glad to reproduce in this book.

" I remember when I was with Miss Atkinson in 1818," writes Mrs. Lefroy, " we used often to walk to Sloane Street where her brother lived and to reach this our walk lay across the Five Fields, Chelsea."

" Now for a little more of the life in St. Stephen's Court or Exchequer Court, or Speaker's Court as we used to write in full after our names in the beginning of our lesson books and there were reasons for these optional addresses. First because the whole pile of ancient buildings which included the Houses of Parliament was the old Palace of Westminster and its Chapel St. Stephen. It was lent by the crown for the use of Parliaments the chapel being assigned for the House of Commons to sit in. The upper part was cut off by a ceiling, so making the groined roof and the upper part of the Gothic windows part of a loft. The upper storey was frequented by ladies who had itching ears for the Debates ; and tickets of admission were granted by the Speaker or M.P.'s. The ladies looked down through peep-holes in the green baize screen which encircled the aperture over the chandelier of wax candles and one could see fairly well by glances to the right and left the Treasury Bench and its *vis-a-vis* with the Speaker on his elevated chair and the three clerks at the table in front of him. Our dear Father sat centre of the three in his silk gown and powdered wig. Mr. Ley on his right, Mr. William Ley on his left.

" We were very much pleased when sometimes Papa came in to his late tea and said that a good debate was coming on unexpectedly, no doubt the roof was pretty vacant and we might have tickets and go there.

" Underneath the House of Commons is the groined cript of the desecrated chapel, and it was used by the Speaker for his State dinners."

Many an imposing procession by land or by water, on the occasion of some marked public event, was witnessed by " little Anne " and is recorded in the *Recollections*. Writing of Lord Mayor's Day she says : " We thought very much of it and Mrs. Wilde had a party of children to see the sight from the windows of their house. Upstairs and down we quite filled every space with our faces.

" The new Lord Mayor came from Temple Bar Water gate in his gold Barge, rowed by at least twenty men in scarlet and gold with red oars. The cabin end of the Barge like a Gondola had windows with gilded frames, through which was visible a grand cold collation, a forest of flags on the top, surrounding the citizens, Aldermen and others in their furred robes. A band of music attended in a lesser barge and there were 5 or 6 others belonging to the various city companies, much gilded. The Fishmongers', I remember, had a grand gold Dolphin at the prow. These barges waited about for an hour or two whilst the Mayor and his retinue were at the Exchequer taking their oaths of allegiance and eating lunch. ' Sprats ' was the orthodox old-fashioned refreshment and before starting from the city, mutton-broth, etc., had been the sustainer for the passage by water. The Lord Mayor's feast at Guildhall concluded this day of many meals."

Postage was a serious matter in those days, and as an alleviation " franking " was allowed. Mrs. Lefroy tells us that M.P.'s could frank ten letters a day while the three clerks at the " Table " could frank an unlimited number. These were privileges for the well-to-do ; about twenty years later Penny Postage brought privileges for the poor.

Speaking again of personal matters Mrs. Lefroy tells us that when she was only five years old she was taken by her father and mother on a series of driving tours in order to visit our beautiful cathedrals, her father looking upon this as a part of her education.

The gig in which the family travelled is thus described in the *Recollections* :

BOSTON STUMP

From the old Copperplate Magazine

" The gig was a comfortable large yellow affair on two wheels with a hood to move up and down and a projection behind called the Sword-case.

" I think we went about 24 miles a day ; All this was done with our one horse Whitefoot who had a light bay coat. We rested always on a Sunday and perhaps one other day when there was much to be seen.

" When we visited the high tower of the church at Boston, called ' Boston stump,' I remember we were on the tower as Sir Joseph Banks with his wife and sister passed through the town to their Park close by and the bells nearly stunned us. We were invited to spend a day and night there, and I well remember that in the Park there were kangaroos hopping about, come from the newly discovered ' New Holland,' also black swans with red bills.

" Durham too (we visited) with Mr. Southey from Keswick.

" I think by the time I was eight years old I had visited all the cathedrals in England and Wales."

Of Lincoln Cathedral she wrote in her diary in a large round hand : " This is the finest Cathedral I have seen," and it remained her favourite, for later on when she drew up, at her father's suggestion, a Table of the comparative dimensions and elevations of our English Cathedrals on the principle that if all were

By the year 1803, however, he had wisely determined to give himself wholly up to his natural bent,
and we find that his books, consisting of poetry,
romance and biography, were greatly appreciated by
the public. Southey quitted London, and after
forming various other plans which were not carried
out he took up his residence at Keswick, where he
shared a house—Greta Hall—with the Coleridges,
a temporary arrangement at first but which proved
a settlement for life.

On Southey being first invited to make the Rickmans' house his regular London resort, Rickman
had written to him in the following comical way :
" I understand Longman and Rees affect to furnish
tea and toast once a week to hungry Literati. A
blessed society it must be, considering the fashionable
sort of conversation among that class of beings ;
abstraction of all sorts, information of no sort ; envy,
murmurings and meanness. The day of little men
is come."

Southey writing to a friend about Rickman
remarks : " His manners are stoical ; they are like
the husk of a coconut, but his inner nature is like
the milk within its kernel. When I go to London
I am always his guest. He gives me but half a hand
when he welcomes me at the door, but I have his whole
heart,—and there is not that thing in the world which
he thinks would serve or gratify me that he does not

THE SANCTUARY

From a sketch by Anne Rickman, afterwards Mrs. Lefroy

do unless it be something which he thinks I can do as well myself."

In Southey's *Life* we have many pretty glimpses of his children. Writing to his younger brother, Lieutenant Southey, in 1808, he says : " We have got the prettiest kitten you ever saw—a dark tabby— and we have christened her by the heathenish name of Dido. You would be very much diverted to see her hunt Herbert all round the kitchen, playing with his little bare feet, which she just pricks at every pat, and the faster he moves back the more she paws them, at which he cries, ' Naughty Dido ' and points to his feet, ' hurt, hurt, naughty Dido.' Presently he feeds her with comfits, which Dido plays with a while, but soon returns to her old game."

Writing to his intimate friend, Grosvenor Bedford, he says : " If Gifford could see me by this fireside, where like Nicodemus one candle suffices me in a large room, he would see a man in a coat still more threadbare than his own. When he wrote his *Imitation*, working hard and getting little—a bare maintenance, and hardly that ; writing poems and history for posterity with his whole heart and soul ; our daily progression is learning, not so learned as he is poor, not so poor as proud, not so proud as happy. Grosvenor, there is not a lighter-hearted nor a happier man upon the face of this wide world.

" Your godson thinks I have nothing to do but

habitually cheerful (than myself), but this belief is the root which gives life to all and holds all fast."

Southey's fame as a writer was steadily gaining ground, and in 1807 we are told by the Editor of his *Life* that Scott, always a true friend to Southey, had written proposing that he should write for the *Edinburgh Review*, in spite of the adverse criticism in that journal of *Thalaba* and *Madoc*, adding " that notwithstanding the flippancy of these attacks Jeffrey had the most sincere respect for his person and talents."

Southey wrote to Scott (December 8, 1807) :

" I am very much obliged to you for the offer which you make concerning the *Edinburgh Review*, and am fully sensible of your friendliness and the advantages which it holds out. I bear as little ill-will to Jeffrey as he does to me and attribute whatever . . . pert things he has said of me . . . to the habit which he has acquired of taking it for granted that the writer is, by virtue of his office, superior to every writer whom he chooses to summon before him. The reviewals of *Thalaba* and *Madoc* do in no degree influence me. Setting all personal feelings aside, the objections which weigh with me against bearing any part in this journal are these : I have scarcely one opinion in common with it upon any subject. Jeffrey is for peace, and is endeavouring to frighten the people into it. I am for war as long as Bonaparte lives. . . . My feelings are still less in unison with him than my opinions. . . . That sort of bitterness in which he indulges, which tends directly to wound a man in his feelings and injure him in his fame and fortune (Montgomery is a case in point) appears to me utterly inexcusable." And writing soon afterwards to a friend about a slashing review upon a novel that had just appeared he remarks : " That book of Miss Swansin's is, I daresay, very bad both in manners and morals, yet had it fallen into my hands, I think I could have told her so in such a spirit that she herself would have believed me, and might have profited by the censure. The same quantity of rain which would clear a flower of its blights will, if it falls heavier and harder, wash the roots bare and beat the blossoms to the ground."

About this time (1817) we learn that Southey " had an offer of a share in the profit of the *Times* with an income of £2,000 if he were willing to remove to London and to write for that paper ; an offer that was at once declined." Southey acted wisely, for he knew well that he enjoyed advantages in the beautiful and health-giving surroundings of his Keswick home that outweighed any amount of income to be obtained by living in London. He had an extraordinary capacity for brain work, but it needed a life of quiet which he could arrange for himself to enable him to carry out his many projects.

Southey remarks in a letter to his brother : " Will you not laugh to hear that I have actually been employed all the morning in making arrangements for a subscription ball at Keswick ? I !—very I ! your brother R. S. To what vile purpose may he come ? It was started by Harry and Miss Charter at the theatre (for we have a strolling company at the ale-house here) and he and I and General Peche have settled it ; and all Cumberland will now envy the gaieties of Keswick. Mrs. General insisted upon my opening the ball with her. I advised her, as she was for performing impossibilities, to begin with turning the wind, before she could hope to turn me, so I shall sip my tea and talk with the old folks some hour or so, and then steal home to write *Madoc*, drink my solitary glass of punch and get to bed at a good Christian-like hour—as my father, and no doubt his father, did before me."

" In one of Lamb's letters to Coleridge," Barry Cornwall tells us when comparing his friend's merits with those of Southey, " Southey," he declares, " has no pretensions to vie with you in the sublime of poetry but he tells a plain story better."

Southey had a strong feeling for dramatic effect, which came out with special force in such poems as the *Inchcape Bell* and *After Blenheim*.

He had a very high opinion of Wordsworth's gifts both as a poet and a man. " I have known him," he writes to a friend, " for nearly twenty years and for about half that time intimately. The strength and the character of his mind you see in the *Excursion*, and his life does not bely his writings." And then he goes on to predict that posterity will rank him as equal to Milton. " Jeffrey I hear has written what his admirers call a crushing review of the *Excursion*. He might as well seat himself upon Skiddaw and fancy that he crushed the mountain."

Several portraits were taken of Wordsworth, but few of them seem to have been successful. Southey writes to a friend : " Hazlitt has been here—a man of real genius. He has made a very fine portrait of Coleridge for Sir George Beaumont which is said to be in Titian's manner. He has also painted Wordsworth, but so dismally that one of his friends on seeing it exclaimed ' At the gallows—deeply affected by his deserved fate—yet determined to die like a man.' "

Southey's poem of *Roderick* had just been published in February 1815, and he wrote on the occasion :

" The sale of *Roderick* is what I expected, neither better nor worse. It is also just what I should desire if profit were a matter of indifference to me, for I am perfectly certain that great immediate popularity can only be obtained by those faults which fall in with the humour of the times and which are of course ultimately fatal to the poems that contain them."

CHAPTER V

MUSICAL GATHERINGS

WE hear of many a pleasant gathering in the Rickmans' house when often members of the Burney family were present. " There was a cousin Mr. Edward Burney," writes Mrs. Lefroy, " very musical, as was the old Mus. Doc. so there was a very Burney respect for music and Sally (Burney) learnt thorough Bass and played classic music in a very professional manner. . . . I remember a famous quartett played by this clique and once they met at our house, Edward Burney and a very famous Dutch violinist Phillips, a barrister, and Alsager with violon-cellos and double Bass, I can see them now in my mind's eye and we had a party of friends. . . . Mrs. Sharon Turner the Historian's wife, very bright and handsome with gold tissue twisted round her head as a turban, and Mrs. Anthony White, the very handsome wife of the eminent Surgeon. She was in dark green velvet and a white satin skirt with gold thread embroidery. The wife of Mr. Alsager was a young Dutch lady, a beauty whom he had married late in life. I should tell you that amongst these beauties Mrs. Burney with her small thin figure and pale face, in black velvet and good lace, older than all the rest, had an air of dignity, and her little foot was remarkably well supported by an exquisite black satin French slipper."

The name of Edward Burney is well known to those who are familiar with Fanny Burney's Diaries. But during the years when they were written he was known as an artist rather than as a musician. It was he who painted the best portraits of Fanny Burney and who when *Evelina* had obtained a great success made some very pretty drawings which were engraved for illustrations in a new edition. His was a singularly attractive character and it has been immortalized by Charles Lamb in an Essay entitled " Valentine's Day."

After describing some Valentines of a trivial order Elia goes on to say :

" All Valentines are not foolish ; and I shall not easily forget thine, my kind friend (if I may have leave to call you so) E. B.—E. B. lived opposite a young maiden whom he had often seen, unseen, from his parlour window in C——e Street. She was all joyousness and innocence, and just of an age to enjoy receiving a Valentine, and just of a temper to

bear the disappointment of missing one with good
humour. E. B. is an artist of no common powers ;
in the fancy parts of designing, perhaps inferior to
none ; his name is known at the bottom of many a
well-executed vignette in the way of his profession,
but no further ; for E. B. is modest, and the world
meets nobody half-way. E. B. meditated how he
could repay this young maiden for many a favour
which she had done him unknown ; for when a
kindly face greets us, though but passing by, and
never knows us again, nor we it, we should feel it
as an obligation : and E. B. did. This good artist
set himself at work to please the damsel. It was
just before Valentine's day three years since. He
wrought, unseen and unsuspected, a wondrous work.
We need not say it was on the finest gilt paper with
borders—full, not of common hearts or heartless
allegory, but all the prettiest stories of love from Ovid,
and older poets than Ovid (for E. B. is a scholar).
There was Pyramus and Thisbe, and be sure Dido
was not forgot, nor Hero and Leander, and swans
more than sang in Cayster, with mottoes and fanciful
devices, such as beseemed—a work, in short, of
magic. Iris dipt the woof. This on Valentine's
eve he commended to the all-swallowing indis-
criminate orifice—(O ignoble trust !)—of the common
post ; but the humble medium did its duty, and
from his watchful stand the next morning he saw

the cheerful messenger knock and by and by the precious charge delivered. He saw, unseen, the happy girl unfold the Valentine, dance about, clap her hands, as one after one the pretty emblems unfolded themselves. She danced about, not with light love, or foolish expectations, for she had no lover; or, if she had, none she knew that could have created those bright images which delighted her. It was more like some fairy present; a God-send, as our familiarly pious ancestors termed a benefit received where the benefactor was unknown. It would do her no harm. It would do her good for ever after. It is good to love the unknown. I only give this as a specimen of E. B. and his modest way of doing a concealed kindness."

Among the Rickmans' musical friends was William Ayrton the musical critic and the Director of the King's Theatre in the Haymarket where he brought out Mozart's *Don Giovanni* in 1817. Mrs. Lefroy says "he was rather a fine gentleman and a joke with the set in rusty waistcoats."

Ayrton and Lamb were attached friends in spite of Lamb's inability to appreciate Ayrton's musical gifts. He is "my friend A." in "A Chapter on Ears," from which we would quote the following passage. Elia writes:

"When I say that I have no ear you will understand me to mean—*for music*. . . . I think that

sentimentally I am disposed to harmony ; but organi-
cally I am incapable of a tune.   I have been practising
' *God save the King* ' all my life ; whistling and
humming it over to myself in solitary corners ; and
am not yet arrived, they tell me, within many
quavers of it.   Yet hath the loyalty of Elia never been
impeached.

" I am not without suspicion that I have an
undeveloped faculty for music within me.   For
thrumming in my wild way on my friend A.'s piano,
the other morning, while he was engaged in an adjoining parlour—on his return he was pleased to say,
' *he thought it could not be the maid !* '   On his first
surprise at hearing the keys touched in somewhat an
airy and masterful way, not dreaming of me, his
suspicions had lighted on *Jenny*. But a grace,
snatched from a superior refinement, soon convinced
him that some being—technically perhaps deficient,
but higher informed from a principle common to all
the fine arts—had swayed the keys to a mood which
Jenny with all her (less cultivated) enthusiasm could
never have elicited from them.   I mention this as a
proof of my friend's penetration and not with any
view of disparaging Jenny."

" Ayrton was here yesterday," Lamb writes to
a friend, " he talked on Music, and by having read
Hawkins and Burney recently I was enabled to talk
of Names and show more knowledge than he had

suspected I possessed ; and in the end he begg'd
me to shape my thoughts upon paper, which I did
after he was gone and sent him.

> Some cry up Haydn, some Mozart
> Just as the whim bites.   For my part
> I do not care a farthing candle
> For either of them or for Handel.
> Cannot a man live free and easy
> Without admiring Pergolesi !
> Or through the world with comfort go
> That never heard of Dr. Blow !
>
> .   .   .   .   .
>
> The devil, with his foot so cloven,
> For aught I care, may take Beethoven ;
> And if the bargain does not suit
> I'll throw him Weber in to boot !
>
> .   .   .   .   .
>
> I would not go four miles to visit
> Sebastian Bach—or Batch—which is it ?
> No more I would for Bononcini.
> As for Novello and Rossini
> I shall not say a word to grieve 'em
> Because they're living.   So I leave 'em.

The following postcript to these verses is said to
have been written by Mary Lamb :

> The reason why my brother's so severe,
> Vincentio, is—my brother has no ear ;
> And Caradori her mellifluous throat
> Might stretch in vain to make him learn a note.
> Of common tunes he knows not anything,
> Nor " Rule Britannia " from " God save the King."
> He rail at Handel !   He the gamut quiz !
> I'd lay my life he knows not what it is.
> His spite at music is a pretty whim—
> He loves not it, because it loves not him.

A member of the Burney family, dear to the heart of Charles Lamb, was Martin Burney, a son of the Admiral.

Barry Cornwall writes : " The man whom I found at Lamb's house more frequently than any other person was Martin Burney. Lamb was very much attached to Martin, who was a sincere and able man, although with a very unprepossessing physiognomy. His face was warped by paralysis which affected one eye and one side of his mouth. He was plain and unaffected in manner, very diffident and retiring, yet pronouncing his opinion, when asked to do so, without apology or hesitation. He was a barrister ; and travelled the Western Circuit at the same time as Sir Thomas Wilde (afterwards Lord Truro), whose briefs he used to read before the other considered them. Martin Burney had excellent taste in books ; eschewed the showy and artificial and looked into the sterling qualities of writing. He frequently accompanied Lamb in his visits to friends, and though very familiar with Charles, he always spoke of him with respect as *Mr*. Lamb. . . ."

" It was curious," remarks the writer, " to observe the gradations in Lamb's manner to his various guests ; although it was courteous to all. With Hazlitt he talked as though they met the subject in discussion on equal terms ; with Leigh Hunt he exchanged repartees ; to Wordsworth he was almost respectful ; with Coleridge he was sometimes jocose, sometimes deferring ; with Martin Burney fraternally familiar ; with Manning affectionate ; with Godwin merely courteous ; or if friendly, then in a minor degree."

Leigh Hunt in the *London Journal* tells this story :

" How obstinate M. B. is," observed a visitor.

" He's an excellent fellow," said Lamb, avoiding the point ; " I like M."

" But he's so obstinate," reiterated the speaker.

" Well," replied Lamb, " I *like* a good solid obstinacy. Something may come of it. Besides— there's something to quarrel with. One's blows don't tell upon a fellow who goes whisking about like a ball of worsted, and won't stand up for his own opinion. M.'s a freeholder, and insists upon having his vote."

Martin's nature was so simple and loving, his character so true, as to draw from Lamb this beautiful tribute :

> In all my threadings of this worldly maze
> (And I have watched thee almost from a child)
> Free from self-seeking, envy, low design,
> I have not found a whiter soul than thine.

And in one of his letters Lamb says of Burney that he is " on the top scale of my friendship ladder on which an angel or two are still standing."

Charles Lamb's love of the Temple, which

transpires so often in his writings, is well known, but we would fain quote a few lines of his inspired description of it.

" I was born and passed the first seven years of my life in the Temple," he writes. " Its Church, its Halls, its gardens, its fountains, its river, I had almost said—for in those young years what was the King of rivers to me but a stream that watered our pleasant places ?—these are of my oldest recollections. I repeat, to this day, no verses to myself more frequently or with kindlier emotion, than those of Spenser where he speaks of this spot. Indeed, it is the most elegant spot in the metropolis. What a transition for a countryman visiting London for the first time—the passing from the crowded Strand or Fleet Street, by unexpected avenues, into its magnificent ample squares, its classic green recesses ! What a cheerful liberal look hath that portion of it which from three sides overlooks the greater garden (and) that goodly pile

Of buildings strong albeit of Paper hight

confronting with massy contrast the lighter, older, more fantastically shrouded one named of Harcourt with the cheerful Crown-Office-Row (place of my kindly engendure) right opposite the stately stream which washes the garden-foot with her yet scarcely trade-polluted waters and seems but just weaned

4 INNER TEMPLE LANE
Charles Lamb's Dwelling
By Charles A. Platt

from her Twickenham Naiades ! A man would give something to have been born in such places. What a collegiate aspect has that fine Elizabethan hall where the fountain plays, which I have made to rise and fall how many times ! to the astoundment of the young urchins my contemporaries, who not being able to guess at its recondite machinery were almost tempted to hail the wondrous work as Magic."

These lines occur in the Essay of Elia entitled " The Old Benchers of the Inner Temple." Lamb, fearing he may have treated one of these members with but scanty justice, exhorts the New Benchers of the Temple to cherish him kindly, " for he is himself the kindliest of human creatures," and then he goes on to say: " So may the Winged Horse, your ancient badge and cognizance, still flourish ! So may future Hookers and Seldons illustrate your Church and chambers ! So may the sparrows, in default of more melodious quiristers, hop about your walks ! So may the fresh-coloured and cleanly nursery-maid, who by leave airs her playful charge in your stately gardens, drop her prettiest blushing curtsey as ye pass. . . . So may the younkers of this generation eye you pacing your stately terrace with the same superstitious veneration with which the child Elia gazed on the Old Worthies that solemnized the parade before ye ! "

CHAPTER VI

POETS IN GREAT COLLEGE STREET

AT the period of which we are writing two poets were living in Great College Street, Westminster—namely, Shelley and Keats, Shelley at No. 17, and Keats at No. 25. Shelley had recently been expelled from Oxford for publishing a treatise in favour of Atheism. It seems to us that his painful views on religious subjects were probably due to the " brutal treatment " received by him when a sensitive child at school, for how could he know anything of a God of love if his teachers, calling themselves Christians, could treat him as they did ?

Southey met Shelley for the first time in Keswick in 1812, and writes of him to a friend : " He is just what I was in 1794. . . . At present he has got to the Pantheistic stage of philosophy and in the course of a week I expect he will be a Berkeleyan, for I have put him upon a course of Berkeley. It has surprised him a good deal to meet, for the first time in his life, with a man who perfectly understands him and does him full justice. I tell him that all the difference between us is that he is nineteen and I am thirty-seven, and I daresay it will not be very long before I shall succeed in convincing him that he may be a true philosopher, and do a great deal of good with 6000 a year (which he possesses) but the thought of which troubles him a great deal more at present than ever the want of sixpence (for I have known such a want) did me."

Cowden Clarke in his *Recollections of Writers* tells us how a young daughter of Vincent Novello (whom he afterwards married) first saw Shelley. " The poet had been calling on her parents, she was told, and on his leaving she watched for the opening of the street door and then quickly climbed on to a chair that she might catch sight of the young poet spoken so highly of by her father and mother—Percy Bysshe Shelley. She saw him move lightly down the two or three stone steps from the entrance, and as he went past the front of the house he suddenly looked up at it, revealing fully to view his beautiful poet's face with its clear blue eyes surmounted by an aureole of gold brown hair."

Mrs. Cowden Clarke (Victoria Novello) has recorded some of her early recollections of Lamb among children.

He had carried to the Novello's nursery, it seems, a jar of preserved ginger. " Long did the remembrance

E

remain in the family," she writes, " of that delicious rarity and of the mode in which Mr. Lamb stalked up and down the passage with a mysterious harbinger-ing look and stride muttering something that sounded like conjuration, holding the precious jar under his arm and feigning to have found it stored away in a dark chimney somewhere near."

Cowden Clarke gives us pleasant glimpses of this group of young men of genius with whom he was on terms of friendship.

He tells us of "the exquisite evenings of Mozartian operatic and chamber music at Vincent Novello's own house where Leigh Hunt, Shelley, Keats and the Lambs were invited guests, and describing them more particularly on a certain occasion he writes : " Keats with his picturesque head leaning against the instru-ment, one foot raised on his knee and smoothed beneath his hands, Leigh Hunt with his jet black hair and expressive mouth, Shelley with his poet's eyes and brown curls, and Lamb with his spare figure and earnest face."

He tells also of " the brilliant supper parties at the alternate dwellings of the Novellos, the Hunts and the Lambs who had mutually agreed that bread and cheese with celery and Elia's immortalized ' Lutheran Beer ' were to be the only cates provided." He speaks also of the picnic repasts enjoyed together by appointment in the fields that lay spread in great

GREAT COLLEGE STREET AND ST. DUNSTAN'S WALL
By Nora Scott

breadths and luxuriance between the west end of Oxford Street and the western slope of Hampstead Hill.

In those days Cowden Clarke was an usher in his father's school at Enfield, and he tells us that "he often walked up to London to enjoy a visit to the Theatre where Kean and Kemble and Miss O'Neal were then acting." On returning home at night, "dark and solitary enough were the green lanes," he says, "that lay between Holloway and Enfield—through picturesque Hornsey, rural Wood Green and hedge-rowed Winchmore Hill—when traversed in the small hours past midnight."

Keats was studying medicine whilst lodging in Westminster, and he had already been apprenticed to a surgeon.

"He attended the usual Hospital Lectures," remarks a biographer, "and proved himself to be a capable if fitful student of his profession. But poetry was the only thing for which he really cared. All other pursuits were mean and tame." Happily he soon gave up the idea of following the medical profession, and in 1817, when he was only twenty-one, published his first poems. They were soon followed by *Endymion*. Leigh Hunt, to whom Keats had been introduced by Cowden Clarke, lent a friendly hand, we are told, to their appearing before the public.

He was attached to both Shelley and Keats, but

his friendship for Shelley was of a calmer and more peaceful order than that with Keats. Keats's ill-health made him morbidly sensitive and even suspicious at times of his friend's actions, but Leigh Hunt fully recognized the cause of this, and bore no malice. He writes in his Autobiography : " I could not love him so deeply as I did Shelley. That was impossible, but my affection was only second to the one which I entertained for that heart of hearts."

Crabb Robinson writes in his Diary, after reading the beginning of Keats's *Hyperion* : " Really a piece of great promise. There is a force, a wildness and an originality in the works of this young poet which, if his perilous journey to Italy does not destroy him, promises to place him at the head of the next genera-tion of poets." Lamb places him next to Words-worth—not meaning any comparison, for they are dissimilar. And again, after reading a volume of his poems, Crabb Robinson remarks : " Great feeling and a powerful imagination are shown in this little volume."

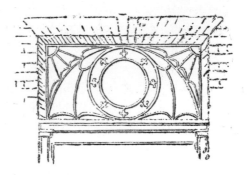

CHAPTER VII

A PAINTER ESSAYIST

A PROMINENT member of Charles Lamb's clique of friends was William Hazlitt, whose writings give us charming glimpses of Lamb's Wednesday or Thursday evening gatherings.

"There was Lamb himself," he writes, "the most delightful, the most provoking, the most witty and sensible of men. He always made the best pun and the best remark in the course of the evening. His serious conversation, like his serious writings, is his best. No one can ever stammer out such fine piquant deep eloquent things in half a dozen sentences as he does. His jests scald like tears and he probes a question with a play upon words. What a keen laughing hairbrained vein of homefelt truth ! What choice venom ! How often did we cut into the haunch of letters ! How we skimmed the cream of criticism ! How we picked out the marrow of authors ! . . . I cannot say that the party at L(amb's) were all of one description. Wit and good fellowship

was the motto inscribed over the door. When a
stranger came in, it was not asked, ' Has he written
anything ? '—we were above that pedantry ; but we
waited to see what he could do. If he could take a
hand at piquet he was welcome to sit down. . . .
But we abhorred insipidity, affectation and fine
gentlemen. There was one of our party who never
failed to mark ' two for his nob at cribbage,' and he
was thought no mean person. This was Ned
P(hillips), and a better fellow in his way breathes not.
There was R(ickman) who asserted some incredible
matter of fact as a likely paradox, and settled all
controversies by an *ipse dixit*, a *fiat* of his will, ham-
mering out many a hard theory on the anvil of his
brain—the Baron Munchausen of politics and practical
philosophy :—there was Captain B(urney) who had
you at an advantage by never understanding you ;
there was Jim White the author of *Falstaff's Letters*—
there was Ayrton who sometimes dropped in, the
Will Honeycomb of our set—and Mrs. R(ickman),
who being of a quiet turn, loved to hear a noisy
debate."

About this time Mary Lamb wrote to a friend :
" Yesterday evening we were at Rickmans' and who
should we find there but Hazlitt. . . . We were very
much pleased because we dearly love our friends
to be respected by our friends."

Leigh Hunt would sometimes join these gatherings. Hazlitt writes of him : " He has a great flow of pleasantry and delightful animal spirits ; but his hits do not tell like L(amb's), you cannot repeat them the next day. He sits at the head of a party with great gaiety and grace ; has an elegant manner and turn of features, is never at a loss . . . has continual sportive sallies of wit or fancy, tells a story capitally, mimics an actor or an acquaintance to admiration . . . manages an argument adroitly :—if he has a fault it is that he does not listen so well as he speaks."

Hazlitt goes on to say : " The art of conversation is the art of hearing as well as of being heard. Authors in general are not good listeners. . . . Some of the best talkers are on this account the worst company. . . . It is sometimes wonderful to see how a person who has been entertaining or tiring a company by the hour together, drops his countenance as if he had been shot, or had been seized with a sudden lockjaw, the moment any one interposes a single observation. The best converser, however, I know is the best listener, I mean Mr. Northcote the painter. Painters by their profession are not bound to shine in conversation, and they shine the more. He lends an ear to an observation as if you had brought him a piece of news and enters into it with as much avidity and earnestness as if it interested him personally. . . . If he repeats an old remark or story it is with the same freshness and point as for the first time. . . . His look is a continual ever-varying history piece of what passes in his mind. His face is a book. There need no marks of interjection or interrogation to what he says." Crabb Robinson was among the happy frequenters of the Lambs' Wednesday (afterwards Thursday) evening gatherings and also saw the Lambs and their special clique of friends on other occasions. He has jotted down many an interesting circumstance connected with them in his Diaries.

On one occasion he writes : " At 7 went to Alsager's. . . . There I met the Lambs, Hazlitt, Burrett, Ayrton, Coulon, Sly and Godwin. I enjoyed the evening. Hazlitt was argumentative, acute and interesting. I had no conversation with him but I enjoyed his conversation with others. Lamb was good-humoured and droll with great originality as usual."

On another occasion he writes : " My print of Leonardo da Vinci, ' La Vierge aux Rochers,' was brought home framed. I took it to Miss Lamb as a present. She was much pleased with it and so was Lamb. . . . I took tea with him. . . . We played a rubber of whist. Lamb was in great good humour, delighted like a child with his present ; but I am to change the frame for him as all his other frames are black. How Lamb confirms the remark of the childlikeness of genius ! "

WILLIAM HAZLITT
By John Hazlitt
Reproduced by permission of Messrs. Martin Secker and Mr. P. P. Howe

Hazlitt had become a distinguished figure amongst the Essay writers and reviewers of the day, but he had begun his career as a painter ; working in the studio of his brother John Hazlitt, an artist of repute who has handed down to posterity a charming portrait of the child William.

It seems to us that Hazlitt was far more suited by nature and disposition to be a painter than a writer—as far as his own personal happiness was concerned, though the loss of his genius in the World of Letters would have been great indeed had he abandoned that profession.

We read in his Essay " On the Pleasure of Painting " :

" There is a pleasure in painting which none but painters know. In writing you have to contend with the world ; in painting you have only to carry on a friendly strife with Nature. You sit down to your task and are happy. From the moment that you take up the pencil and look at Nature in the face, you are at peace with your own heart. . . . There is no juggling here, no sophistry, no intrigue, no tampering with the evidence, no attempt to make black white or white black ; but you resign yourself into the hands of a greater power, that of Nature, with the simplicity of a child and the devotion of an enthusiast—' study with joy her manner and with rapture taste her style.' You try to set down what

you see, find out your error, and correct it. . . .
Patience grows out of the endless pursuit, and turns
it into a luxury."

And he writes in another Essay : " Perhaps
there is no part of a Painter's life (if one must tell the
secrets of the Prison-house) in which he has more
enjoyment of himself and his art, than that in which,
after his work is over, and with furtive side-long
glances at what he has done, he is employed in washing
his brushes and cleaning his palette for the day.
Afterwards when he gets a servant in livery to do
this for him he may have other and more ostensible
sources of satisfaction, greater splendour, wealth or
fame ; but he will not be so wholly in his art, nor
will his art have such a hold on him, as when he
was too poor to transfer its meanest drudgery to
others. . . .

" One of my first attempts was a picture of my
father, who was then in a green old age with strong
marked features and scarred with the smallpox. I
drew it out with a broad light crossing the face,
looking down with spectacles on, reading. . . . The
sketch promised well. . . . My father was willing
to sit as long as I pleased, for there is a natural desire
in the mind of man to sit for one's picture . . . and
besides his satisfaction in the picture he had some
pride in the artist though he would rather I should
have written a sermon than painted like Rembrandt

or like Raphael. Those winter days with the gleams
of sunshine coming through the chapel windows, and
cheered by the notes of the robin-redbreast in our
garden (that ' ever in the haunch of winter sings ')—
as my afternoon's work drew to a close—were among
the happiest of my life."

In 1802, when the Peace of Amiens had opened
the way to Paris to all lovers of its treasures, Hazlitt,
armed with a commission to make five copies of some
of the celebrated pictures in the Louvre, was enabled
to take the desired journey.

" The first day I got there," he writes, " I was kept
for some time in the French Exhibition Room, and
thought I should not be able to get a sight of the old
masters. I just caught a glimpse of them through the
door (vile hindrance !) like looking out of purgatory
into Paradise—from Poussin's noble mellow-looking
landscapes to where Rubens hung out his gaudy
banner, and down the glimmering vista to the rich
jewels of Titian and the Italian school. At last by
much importunity I was admitted and lost not an
instant in making use of my new privilege. I marched
delighted through a quarter of a mile of the proudest
efforts of the mind of man, a whole creation of
genius, a universe of art.

" Here for four months together I strolled and
studied, and daily heard the warning sound—
' *Quatre heures passées, il faut fermer, Citoyens* '

muttered in coarse provincial French. . . . How often, thou tenantless mansion of god-like magnificence —how often has my heart since gone a pilgrimage to thee ! Where the treasure is, there the heart is also. It is now seventeen years since I was studying in the Louvre (and I have long since given up all thoughts of the art as a profession), but long after I returned, and even still, I sometimes dream of being there again—of asking for the old pictures—and not finding them, or finding them changed, or faded from what they were ; I cry myself awake."

It was said of Hazlitt that although his earnest study of Art had not made him a painter it had enabled him to become a writer. The beauty of nature and of the noble works of the great Masters had entered into his very soul and illuminates all that he has written on these subjects.

We read in one of his Essays, when alluding to the Raphael Cartoons and the Elgin Marbles : " We like those noble outlines of the human face at Hampton Court ; the sustained dignity of the expression ; the broad ample folds of the drapery ; the bold massive limbs ; there is breath and motion in them. . . . We also like the sway of the limbs and negligent grandeur of the Elgin Marbles ; in spite of their huge weight and manly strength, they have the buoyancy of a wave of the sea, with all the ease and softness of flesh."

Hazlitt, however, in spite of his brilliant talents suffered from certain physical defects which caused him to be often misunderstood by strangers. He had an irascible temper and a shy awkward manner, and was further troubled in early life by a stammer.

" It was in after years," we are told, " by the fire-side of the Lambs that his tongue was gradually loosened, and his passionate thoughts found appropriate words . . . there he was thoroughly understood and dexterously cheered by Miss Lamb, whose nice discernment of his first efforts at conversation was dwelt upon by him with affectionate gratitude, even when most out of humour with the world."

Talfourd in alluding to his strange infatuation concerning Napoleon remarks : " On this subject only he was ' eaten up with passion,' on all others he was the fairest, the most candid of reasoners. . . . When in the society of Lamb and one or two others, he talked on his favourite themes of old English books and of old Italian pictures no one's conversation could be more delightful."

Barry Cornwall writes of meeting him for the first time about the year 1816. " He was already well known," he says, " to be a firstrate critic in matters connected with art and the theatre ; and by his associates (some of them not too ready to admit the claims of literary candidates) he was characterized as an acute and profound thinker. His countenance

did not belie this opinion. His figure was indeed
indifferent, and his movements shy and awkward ;
but there was something in his earnest irritable face,
his restless eyes, his black hair, combed backwards
and curling (not too resolutely) about a well-shaped
head, that was very striking. They would have made
an excellent picture. Had the painter whom he most
loved (Titian) been then living, he would have been
well pleased to have had such a countenance whereon
to exercise his art, nor would he have disdained to
hand down to posterity the features of his eloquent
admirer."

When he was still a youth, Hazlitt became
acquainted with Sheridan Knowles—then a lad of
singular promise, and undertook to aid him in his
literary tastes. A son of Sheridan Knowles who
wrote a biography of his father describing this period
remarks : " The tutelage of such a mind was invalu-
able to a lad who, with a strong love for poetry, had
as yet insight only into his own ideas. . . . There is
something very pleasing," he observes, " in the picture
of a young man of Hazlitt's vigorous mind and large
acquaintance with literature, conscious of powers
which would make him a master among men, taking
pains with a boy six years his junior, when he himself
was not well out of his teens, and endeavouring to
enlarge his views and correct his judgment. ' He
loved me,' said my father years afterwards, looking

back to this time, ' taught me as a friend, endearingly praising and condemning, as he saw cause, every little poem which I wrote. There was ore in him and rich, but his maturer friends were blind to it. I saw it. He was a man to whom I could have submitted my life ! ' "

CHAPTER VIII

A PATRIOT POET

THERE was much discontent and disturbance in the country at the period of which we are writing. Parliamentary Reform was sorely needed, but the Government feared any change in the existing system and advocates for reform were looked upon with much suspicion.

Among these advocates were the brothers Leigh Hunt and John Hunt, who had recently started their new paper the *Examiner* expressly for the purpose of promoting reforms of all kinds. They were young enthusiasts and their prospectus evinces much confidence in themselves and their own theories and contempt for their opponents. In the paragraph on Domestic Economy occur the following words : " The man, however high his rank may be, or profuse of interest his connexion, who dares to take advantage of his elevation in society to trample with gayer disdain on the social duties," the " selfish and vulgar cowards " whether jockeys (who run a horse to death) or cock-fighters, or " those miserable ruffians, whether the ornaments of a gaol or the disgracers of a noble house" who "encourage or practise prize-fighting—are not to be spared." . . . Above all no quack doctors. " If the paper cannot be witty or profound, it shall at least never be profligate." "What fine sentiments are these!" (might the casual reader remark), " what very superior persons must the Proprietors be or think themselves!" But the worst of it was that the promises were kept, the sentiments were genuine, and the Hunts were really " superior persons," for their principles were founded on the most elemental canons of truth and justice, and they stuck to them in spite of the most powerful and virulent persecution.* This persecution came to a head in March 1812, on the appearance in the *Examiner* of an article which soon became famous, containing, as it did, a strong denunciation of the character of the Prince Regent in reply to some absurd flatteries relating to him that had just appeared before the public.

We would give a few passages from the article.

" What person unacquainted with the true state of the case would imagine in reading these astounding eulogies that this ' Glory of the People ' . . . this ' Conqueror of hearts ' was the disappointer of hopes ? . . . In short, this ' *delightful, blissful, wise, pleasur-*

* See *Life of Leigh Hunt*, by Monkhouse.

F

able, honourable, virtuous, true and immortal' prince was a violator of his word and a libertine over head and ears in disgrace."

The result of the article was that the brothers Leigh Hunt and John Hunt were sentenced to a period of imprisonment in separate gaols of two years and each of them to a fine of £500—offers to remit the penalties on a promise not to make similar attacks on the Prince Regent in the future were courageously refused. This conduct aroused a widespread sympathy for the Hunts, and when Leigh Hunt was incarcerated in the gaol in Horsemonger Lane and John in that of Clerkenwell, many were the visits they received from the leading men of the time. Leigh Hunt's wife and children were allowed to live with him and he was permitted to continue to edit the *Examiner* from prison, which had come to be regarded as one of the most important political papers of the day. He was honoured on all hands. Byron, we are told, brought him food and his own poems; the philosopher Bentham played at shuttlecock with his children in the prison-yard; while young Shelley at Oxford sent him offers of financial assistance. The painters Wilkie and Haydon and the poet Moore together with Mr. Brougham all eagerly sought the society of the Patriot-Poet, as he had come to be called.

Here it was that Hazlitt first made his acquaintance

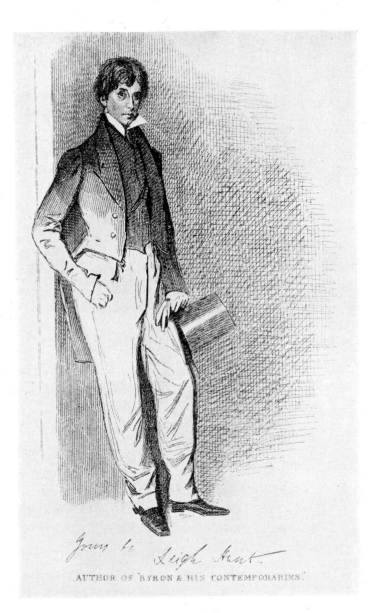

Yours &[?] Leigh Hunt.

AUTHOR OF BYRON & HIS CONTEMPORARIES.

LEIGH HUNT
By Maclise

and found him seated in his prison-room, on " the ceiling of which he had caused a blue sky with white clouds to be painted, while the walls were decorated with trellised roses."

But the most constant of his visitors were the Lambs, who came "in all weathers, hail or sunshine, in daylight and in darkness, even in the dreadful frost and snow of the beginning of 1814." In Leigh Hunt's *Epistle to Charles Lamb*, written about this time, he alludes to those days :

> You'll guess why I can't see the snow-covered streets
> Without thinking of you and your visiting feats,
> When you call to remembrance how you and one more
> When I wanted it most, used to knock at my door.
> For when the sad winds told us rain would come down,
> Or snow upon snow fairly clogged up the town,
> And dun yellow fogs brooded over its white
> So that scarcely a being was seen towards the night,
> Then, then said the lady yclept near and dear,
> " Now mind what I tell you,—the L.'s will be here."
> So I poked up the flame, and she got out the tea,
> And down we both sat, as prepared as could be ;
> And then, sure as fate, came the knock of you two,
> Then the lanthorn, the laugh and the " Well, how d'ye do ? "

As a pendant to this poem we would like to give Lamb's lines addressed to T. L. H. (Thornton Leigh Hunt), the little four-year-old child of Leigh Hunt of whom he was very fond.

> Guileless traitor, rebel mild,
> Convict unconscious, culprit-child,

Gates that close with iron roar
Have been to thee thy nursery door ;
Chains that chink in cheerless cells
Have been thy rattles and thy bells ;
Walls contrived for giant sin
Have hemmed thy faultless weakness in.

But the clouds, that overcast
Thy young morning, may not last,
Soon shall arrive the rescuing hour
That yields thee up to Nature's power,
Nature that so late doth greet thee
Shall in o'er-flowing measure meet thee,
She shall recompense with cost
For every lesson thou hast lost.
Then wandering up thy sire's lov'd hill *
Thou shalt take thy airy fill
Of health and pastime, *Birds shall sing*
For thy delight each May morning . . .
So shall be thy days beguil'd,
Thornton Hunt, my favourite child.

We have said that there was much disturbance throughout the country at this period and that reforms of all kinds were urgently needed. Amongst these was Prison Reform. A contemporary † writing of a visit to the Warwick Gaol says : " In the large yard where the prisoners passed most of the day, I beheld a considerable number of men walking about, unemployed, and all of them in chains. There was a dungeon many feet beneath the yard where the

* Hampstead Hill.
† See *Frederic Hill, an Autobiography of Fifty Years of Reform*, edited by Constance Hill.

wretched prisoners passed the night still in chains."
The same writer remarks : " In the year 1815 I saw
two men standing in the pillory in the Birmingham
Market-place." The pillory is thus described in a
dictionary of the day : " It consists of a frame of
wood erected on posts with movable boards having
holes through which are put the head and hands of
a criminal for punishment." The populace were
accustomed to hurl rotten eggs and all kinds of refuse
at the unhappy culprits, who were, of course, quite
unable to defend themselves in any way. It is said
that when, on one occasion, a man, loved by the people
and regarded as their defender, was sentenced to
stand in the pillory, they pelted him with roses.

The year 1816 was very wet and bad for
agriculture. The corn did not ripen properly and
the price of wheat rose to 100 shillings the quarter.
Great distress prevailed. But a new hope was gaining
ground—as our contemporary writes, " the hope of
Parliamentary Reform. Far off indeed seemed the
possibility of its accomplishment, but many stout-
hearted men were working for that end."

Meanwhile at a great meeting held in Peter's
Field, Manchester, a most arbitrary act was per-
petrated by the yeomanry in firing upon the assembled
crowd although no offence had been committed. Six
persons were killed and a large number wounded.
This was known afterwards as the " Manchester

Massacre." It aroused a strong feeling of indigna-
tion throughout the country.

Rickman, who was a staunch Tory, writes to a
friend in contemptuous terms of the Whig scheme of
Parliamentary Reform, " which the self-complacent
little M.P. for Tavistock introduced," alluding thus
to Lord John Russell ; and he calls Lord Brougham
" a noisy adventurer." Southey also was a Tory,
though of a milder kind. He writes of the Manchester
Massacre : " The Magistrates committed an error in
employing the yeomanry to support the civil power ;
for the yeomanry, after bearing a great deal, lost their
temper, which the disciplined troops would not have
done. The cause of the error is obviously that the
Magistrates thought it less obnoxious to employ
that species of force than the troops—a natural and
pardonable mistake."

He speaks of the possibility of some great dissolu-
tion of Society pending, and goes on to say : " Accord-
ing to all human appearances I should fear the worst,
were it not for an abiding trust in Providence by whose
wise will even our follies are overruled."

CHAPTER IX

BROTHER AND SISTER

THERE was intimacy between the Rickmans and the Lambs. When Mary Lamb suffered from her sad attacks of mental derangement and had to be absent from home for several weeks at a time, Rickman was among the very few friends that Charles turned to for help and comfort.

Rickman (see *Life of John Rickman*) writes one day to Southey : " Yesterday evening, or rather afternoon, C. Lamb came in somewhat abruptly and on sitting down shed some tears. The cause is distressing ; inasmuch as his sister is again seized with an unhappy derangement, and has been therefore compelled to go into custody, away from home ; but as she has usually recovered in about two or three months, we may hope the best. Poor Lamb recovered himself pretty well towards night and slept at my house ; he dines with me to-day, and then hopes that he will be steadied. Write to him," he says to

Southey, " just to amuse him ; he feels dreary and would like a letter from any friend."

After one of her early attacks Charles writes in a poem that ultimately appeared in the *Blank Verse* Volume :

> I am a widowed thing now thou art gone !
> Now thou art gone, my own familiar friend,
> Companion, sister, helpmate, counsellor !
> . . . That honour'd mind become a fearful blank,
> Her senses lock'd up, and herself kept out
> From human sight and converse.

Mary was well aware by premonitory symptoms when an attack was approaching, and she * would " as gently as possible prepare her brother for the duty he must perform, and thus, unless he could stave off the terrible separation till Sunday, oblige him to ask leave of absence from the India Office, as for a day's pleasure—a bitter mockery ! On one occasion Mr. Charles Lloyd met them slowly pacing together a little footpath in the Hoxton fields, both weeping bitterly, and found on joining them that they were taking their solemn way to the accustomed Asylum."

When Mary was first attacked by madness she committed a terrible act. She had been long oppressed by overwork in nursing her sick parents and also in doing needlework to obtain money. She

---

* See *Mary Lamb*, by Mrs. Gilchrist.

had hired a young girl as an apprentice to help in this work, and one day, we are told, " seized with a sudden frenzy, she snatched a knife from the table and pursued the young apprentice round the room, when her Mother interposing, received the fatal stab and died instantly. Mary was totally unconscious of what she had done . . . the father was too feeble in mind for any but a confused impression ; and it was Charles alone who confronted all the anguish and horror of the scene." And it was he who afterwards " sustained the wrecked household and rescued his sister, when reason returned, from the living death of perpetual confinement in a mad-house. He satisfied all the parties who had power to oppose her release by his solemn engagement that he would take her under his care for life ; and he kept his word."

Writing to an intimate friend of his feelings when he was aware that an attack was approaching, Lamb says : " You cannot conceive the misery of such a foresight. . . . My waking life has much of the confusion, the trouble and the obscure perplexity of an ill dream." " Yet nervous, tremulous as he seemed," writes Talfourd, " so slight of frame that he looked only fit for the most placid fortune, when the dismal emergencies which chequered his life arose, he acted with as much promptitude and vigour as if he were strung with Herculean sinews." " Such fortitude in his manners, and such a ravage of suffering in his countenance did he display," says Coleridge, " as went to the hearts of his friends."

Of Mary, Talfourd writes : " Little could anyone observing Miss Lamb in the habitual serenity of her demeanour, guess the calamity in which she had partaken, or the malady which frightfully chequered her life. . . . Her character in all its sweetness was like her brother's ; while by a temper more placid, a spirit of enjoyment more serene, she was enabled to guide, to counsel, to cheer him and to protect him on the verge of the mysterious calamity from the depths of which she rose so often unruffled to his side." Talfourd goes on to say: " In all her thoughts and feelings she was most womanly—keeping under even undue subordination to her notion of a woman's province, an intellect of rare excellence, which flashed out when the restraints of gentle habit and humble manner were withdrawn by the terrible force of disease. Though her conversation in sanity was never marked by smartness or repartee . . . it was otherwise in her madness."

Lamb in a letter to a friend speaks of " her pouring out memories of all the events and persons of her younger days," " but he does not mention," remarks Talfourd, " what I am able, from repeated experiences, to add, that her ramblings often sparkled with brilliant description and shattered beauty. She

CHARLES LAMB
By Hazlitt

MARY LAMB
By Cary

would fancy herself in the days of Queen Anne or George the First ; and describe the brocaded dames and courtly manners, as though she had been bred among them, in the best style of the old comedy. It was all broken and disjointed so that the hearer could remember little of her discourse, but the fragments were like the jewelled speeches of Congreve, only shaken from their settings."

Charles writes to a friend of his sister : " Mary has been ill and gone from home these five weeks yesterday. She has left me very lonely and very miserable. I stroll about, but there is no rest but at one's own fireside, and there is no rest for me there now. . . . The return of her disorder has been frightfully soon this time, with scarce a six-months' interval. I am almost afraid my worry of spirits about the E. I. House was partly the cause of her illness ; but one always imputes it to the cause next at hand, more probably it comes from some cause we have no control over or conjecture of. It eats sad great slices out of the time, the little time we shall have to live together. . . . (But) she has begun to show some favourable symptoms"; and he adds more cheerfully : " By God's blessing in a few weeks we may be taking our meal together, or sitting in the front row of the pit at Drury Lane, or taking our evening walk past the theatres, to look at the outside of them at least, if not to be tempted in. Then we could not help, however, smiling at the phantom of wealth which her dear imagination had conjured up." . . . " It is true we were happier when we were poorer," he says to her, " but we were also younger. . . . That we had much to struggle with, as we grew up together, we have reason to be most thankful. It strengthened and knit our compact closer. We could never have been what we have been to each other, if we had always had the sufficiency which you now complain of."

" We are both great readers in different directions. While I am hanging over, for the thousandth time, some passage in old Burton, or one of his strange contemporaries, she is abstracted in some modern tale of adventure, whereof our common reading table is daily fed with assiduously fresh supplies. She must have a story—well, ill or indifferently told— so there be life stirring in it and plenty of good or evil accidents, (while) out-of-the-way humour and opinions—heads with some diverting twist in them— the oddities of authorship please me most."

" We are both inclined to be a little too positive," he remarks, " and I have observed the result of our disputes to be almost uniformly this—that in matters of fact, dates and circumstances it turns out that I was in the right and my cousin in the wrong. But where we have differed upon moral points ; upon something proper to be done, or let alone ; whatever

THE TEMPLE AND TEMPLE STAIRS

heat of opposition or steadiness of conviction, I set out with, I am sure always in the long run to be brought over to her way of thinking."

When Charles and Mary Lamb were writing *The Tales from Shakespeare*, Mary wrote to a friend : " Charles has written *Macbeth*, *Othello*, *King Lear*, and has begun *Hamlet ;* you would like to see us as we often sit writing on our table (but not on one cushion sitting) like Hermia and Helena in the *Midsummer Night's Dream ;* or rather like an old literary Darby and Joan, I taking snuff and he groaning all the while and saying he can make nothing of it, which he always says till he is finished, and then he finds he has made something of it." *

No sooner were *The Tales from Shakespeare* finished, we are told, than Mary Lamb began to consider what subject she should choose for a new volume of stories for children, and in about a year's time *Mrs. Leicester's School* appeared before the public. Of the ten stories, seven are written by Mary Lamb and three by Charles. It is a singularly attractive little book, and it was thus spoken of by Coleridge to a friend many years after its coming out : " It at once soothes and amuses me," he said, " to think— nay to know—that the time will come when this little volume of my dear and well-nigh oldest friend, Mary Lamb, will be not only enjoyed, but acknow-

* See *Mary Lamb*, by Mrs. Gilchrist.

ledged as a rich jewel in the treasury of our permanent English literature, and I cannot help running over in my mind the long list of celebrated writers, astonishing geniuses, Novels, Romances, Poems, Histories and dense Political Economy quartos which, compared with *Mrs. Leicester's School*, will be remembered as often and prized as highly as Wilkie's and Glover's Epics and Lord Bolingbroke's Philosophies compared with *Robinson Crusoe*." *

Crabb Robinson writes to Dorothy Wordsworth after Lamb had suffered from a temporary illness : " If you look into the last *New Monthly Magazine* you will be delighted by perceiving that Charles Lamb is himself again. His peculiar mixture of wit and fancy is to be found there in all its charming individuality. No one knows better than he the proportion of earnestness and gaiety for his undefinable compositions."

Perhaps it was the tenderness of Lamb's heart that rendered his charm indefinable—a tenderness connected with the love affair of his youth and that had an influence over his whole life. All that we hear of " the gentle Alice with the fair hair " makes us know him better. We should like to close this chapter with the last lines of his " Dream Children."

The little ones, which seemed to be his very own, had gathered around him to hear stories of their

* See *Mary Lamb*, by Mrs. Gilchrist.

forbears when they, too, were young. " They asked me to tell them some stories about their pretty dead mother. Then I told how for seven long years, in hope sometimes, sometimes in despair, yet persisting ever, I courted the fair Alice W——n, and, as much as children could understand, I explained to them what coyness and difficulty and denial meant in maidens—when suddenly, turning to Alice, the soul of the first Alice looked out at her eyes with such a reality of representation, that I became in doubt of them that stood there before me, or whose that bright hair was ; and while I stood gazing, both the children gradually grew fainter to my view, receding and still receding till nothing at last but two mournful features were seen in the uttermost distance, which, without speech, strangely impressed upon me the effects of speech : ' We are not of Alice, nor of thee, nor are we children at all. The children of Alice call Bertrum father. We are nothing ; less than nothing and dreams. We are only what might have been, and must wait upon the tedious shores of Lethe millions of ages before we have existence and a name,' and immediately awakening I found myself quietly seated in my bachelor arm-chair where I had fallen asleep with the faithful Bridget unchanged by my side."

G

CHAPTER X

A ROYAL SUFFERER

AT the period of which we are writing, when rejoicings were annually made on the occasion of the King's birthday and gay processions formed by land and by water in his honour as witnessed by " little Anne," the old King himself was in a sad and suffering state.

We are told in the history of those times * that " his mind continually brooded on his mental derangements of former times, and he applied himself to the mournful task of making a selection from the works of his favourite composer, Handel, of such passages as were descriptive either of madness or blindness, which selection was, at his express desire, communicated through the Duke of Cambridge and performed at the Concert of Ancient Music. Among the passages selected by the King were a representation of madness caused by love in the Opera of *Samson* and the lamentation of Jephthah at the loss

* See *Life and Reign of George III*, by J. Heneage Jesse.

of his daughter. The performance is described as having been singularly impressive and affecting ; more especially when the striking up of ' God save the King ' recalled to the minds of the audience the sufferings of the stricken Monarch."

" It was towards the end of this month (of May) that the inhabitants of Windsor, for the last time, beheld amongst them the familiar Kingly form, with which, from the earliest years, nearly one and all of them had been acquainted. Rumours," writes a contemporary, " went forth that the King was better. On Sunday night, Windsor was in a fever of excitement at the authorized report that the next day the physicians would allow his Majesty to appear in public. On that Monday morning it was said that his saddle-horse was to be got ready. We crowded to the Park and the Castle yard. The favourite horse was there. The venerable man, blind but steady, was soon in the saddle, as I had often seen him— a hobby-groom at his side with a leading-rein. He rode through the Little Park to the Great Park. The bells rang and the troops fired a *feu de joie*. The King returned to the Castle within an hour. He was never again seen without those walls."

We have a glimpse of the poor King in his strange and isolated condition from an unexpected quarter, namely that of the Prince Regent. There was an estrangement between the father and son as is well known, but the circumstances of their meeting were so deeply pathetic that for once the Prince was moved to real feeling. The affair is recorded by the Contesse de Boigne in her *Mémoires*, who, together with her parents the Marquis and Marquise d'Osmond, were often entertained by the Prince in his residence the Pavilion at Brighton.

" I remember," she writes, " having been deeply interested in the conversation one evening when the Regent described to us a recent visit he had paid to the King his father whom he had not seen for several years. The Queen and the Duke of York, who were entrusted with the care of his person, were the only people allowed to see him. I use the word see," she adds, " for no one ever spoke to him. The sound of a voice known or unknown threw him into such a state of agitation that days and even weeks were required to allay it. He was tended with the utmost care, but all was done in profound silence. By this means it was found possible to give him a certain amount of tranquillity. He was totally blind.

" An illness of the Queen's having prevented her from carrying on her affectionate duties, the Regent had taken her place.

" He told us," continues the Contesse, " he was conducted into a large room where, separated from him by a row of arm-chairs, he perceived his venerable father dressed as usual, but the head completely bald and wearing a long white beard which fell over his breast. He was evidently presiding (in imagination) over a State Council, and was addressing Mr. Pitt in perfectly reasonable terms. Apparently some objections were made, for he had the air of listening, and then, after a few moments of silence, he resumed his discourse, insisting further on his own opinion. He then invited another Councillor to speak and listened to him in the same way, and again to a third, whom he addressed by his own name. Finally he announced, in Official terms, that the Council was at an end, and calling his Page to attend him went to visit his children. To these he talked for a long while, especially to the Princess Amelia, his favourite, whose recent and sudden death had greatly contributed to cause the increase of the King's malady. (But he was not conscious of the affair for long.) On quitting her he said : ' I must go soon to the Queen, you know she does not like me to be away from her for long.'

" He then carried out this idea and returned to the Queen. All these walks to and fro were taken leaning on the arm of his page and without leaving the room. After a short conversation with the Queen he rose and went quite alone, although closely followed by his attendant, to the piano, where he began to improvise music or to play from memory the music of Handel, accompanying it by singing in a voice as touching as it was sonorous. This talent for music, an Art which he had always loved passionately, was singularly increased since he had suffered from his cruel malady.

" The Prince told us that he was informed that this musical séance usually lasted for about three hours ; so, after having listened to it for a long time, he withdrew.

" What was truly remarkable in the conduct of this revered old man was that, although wholly unconscious of the time of day (since he never saw daylight), he had an instinct for method and order which moved him to do each day the same thing at the same time, and which moved him also to place, as in former times, the duties of his Royal position before those of his own family.

" To do the Regent justice," remarks the Contesse de Boigne, " I am bound to say that while giving us this moving account, tears were standing in his eyes and that they flowed down his cheeks when he spoke of his father's voice, singing the fine motets of Handel, and described to us the agonizing restraint he had to put upon himself to prevent his springing forward and folding the venerable musician in his arms."

The old King continued to live for more than six years after this affecting scene took place.*   But at

* See *Life and Reign of George III*, by J. Heneage Jesse.

impr
autu
had i
of M
her /

V
was ;
of Q
on a
Fitzl
happ
com
for l
own
in b
erec
over
see
Hou
Alde
with
a co
roug

]
resp
pres
call
I he

12 o'clock on the night of the 29th of January, 1820, the tolling of the great bell of St. Paul's Cathedral announced to the inhabitants of London that the afflicted monarch, who had ruled over them for sixty years, had ceased to exist. . . .

" During the King's long estrangement from the world, he had never been forgotten by his subjects. Their sympathies and prayers had been with him in his living tomb, and when he expired they mourned him as a father.

" The funeral took place at Windsor, amidst much pomp and ceremony, on the night of the 16th of February, when, at 9 o'clock, the long mournful procession moved towards St. George's Chapel, accompanied by the sound of the muffled drums, mingled with the minute-guns and the tolling of the death-bell. . . . When the funeral service was over and the coffin had been lowered into the grave, and the dust thrown upon it, Garter-King-at-Arms proclaimed the titles of the deceased. Once more the volumed tones of the organ pealed along the vaulted roof and through the fretted aisles. The mourners rearranged themselves nearly in the order in which they came . . . the soldiers who had lined the aisles extinguished their tapers and retired . . . the solemn ceremony was at an end."

of the King being drunk, a fellow cried out from the shilling gallery—' The Queen ! ' The allusion was caught up and not a word was heard afterwards. The cries for the health of the Queen were uttered from all quarters, and as this demand could not be complied with, not a syllable more of the farce was audible."

The Ministers of George IV endeavoured to restrain the King from going to extreme measures, but in vain. We learn from the Editor of the *Creevey Papers* that " the negociations broke down upon the question of restoring to the Liturgy the name of ' our most gracious Queen Caroline.' " Upon that point the King was inflexible. When Brougham insisted upon it, " You might as easily move Carlton House," said Castlereagh. The ferment out of doors was mounting and spreading. Meetings were got up all over the country to protest against the persecution of the Queen. There was no regular police force in London at that time ; the Guards were relied upon for maintaining public order, but the Guards had shown strong partiality for the Queen against the Government and one battalion was in actual mutiny.

At a debate in the House of Commons upon the King's refusal to restore his consort's name to the Liturgy, Denman used words which found an echo in millions of hearts throughout the realm. It had been suggested by the Treasury Bench that at least without mentioning her name she might be held as included in the general prayer for the royal family. " If her Majesty is included in any general prayer," retorted Denman, " it is in the prayer for all who are desolate and oppressed." *

Many Italian witnesses had been brought over to England to give evidence against the Queen's conduct during her residence in Italy, but they were of a low class and frequently equivocated, so that their evidence was of little value. It is true that the Queen had acted very imprudently and thoughtlessly, but no guilt could be proved against her. Under these circumstances the Ministers had to abandon the trial. Popular feeling on the occasion was expressed by a general illumination, and in the following Session the Commons voted her an annuity of £50,000.

So ended the famous trial, but the King's attitude towards the unhappy Queen remained unchanged, as we shall see presently in the account of the coronation.

Mrs. Lefroy writes : " Opposite to our house on the terrace of New Palace Yard, there used to be, at Election times, the hustings placed in front of the King's Arms hotel. Here Sir Francis Burdett addressed his constituents, and so did Henry Hunt the Radical candidate, and there was a great uproar

* See *Creevey Papers.*

sometimes." Sir Francis Burdett was an ardent advocate of Parliamentary Reform, which was sorely needed at the period of which we are writing, and his eloquent speeches aided the carrying out of many a good measure for the welfare of the people. He was not like Henry Hunt as extremist, for in an account of his Life we read that " he had never desired to see the prerogative of the Monarch or the privileges of the House of Peers invaded." But he suffered much persecution from the Government.

CHAPTER XII

A CORONATION

THE coronation of King George IV was fixed for July 19, 1821, "which was a great event in my memory," writes Mrs. Lefroy, "and as we were just moving from one house to the other we had the advantage of the two being close to the scene. The new dwelling had its whole front fitted up with tiers of seats (covered) with crimson cloth from top to bottom. One storey was apportioned for our use. The other house of ours we put at the disposal of the Government, and it was used as a sleeping-place the night before for the Prime Minister, Lord Sidmouth, and the Marquis of Londonderry. The King himself, with his attendants, slept at the Speaker's (the Royal Palace of Westminster).

"Every house on the Terrace of New Palace Yard was cased as ours with crimson cloth, even on the roofs. I think it must have been at 12 o'clock that the procession was to reach Westminster Abbey from Westminster Hall. . . . It was a great problem how best to reach your seats in the Abbey and in other places that morning, and it was decided in our case that we had better drive up from Epsom (where we were then staying) very early in the morning, get out of the carriage on the Surrey side of Vauxhall Bridge, take a wherry there and row to the water-gate of our garden terrace, next to Mr. Wilde's.

"How well I remember the very early start at 1 o'clock a.m. with a full moon to light us! There was Mamma with Frances and Willy and our two eldest cousins from Landport, Margaret and Frances Tourle, dressed in Ball attire, hair to be dressed in London, with curls in paper under hoods, and then the moon frightened the gay young horses, so that handkerchiefs were tied over their blinkers. It was hot weather (but) I remember it was very fine. We took boat at Vauxhall and we reached our garden gate opening to the Thames at 5 a.m., having observed a line of carriages all along Vauxhall Bridge, with ladies in full dress on their way to their places. A Policeman (watchman) in a red waistcoat received our tickets, and we were amused to be informed 'that no one must touch the flowers,' *our* flowers. This was very satisfactory, only we had a wish to furnish ourselves with our own white lilies to add to the blue larkspur that we had brought up with us for wreaths in our hair. I suppose an explanation took place, for we wore the lilies, and then we panted a little over the jeopardy of our muslin frocks which were in the wardrobe of Mamma's dressing-room, which could only be reached through her bedchamber, in which the valet was dressing Lord Sidmouth's hair! It seemed as if it would never be complete. Indeed it was so long that at last we were hurried through and Mamma dressed us there, blue sashes and white kid shoes, and we emerged again by his mild pale smile unharmed.

"We soon passed through our unfurnished house and joined our friends to whom Papa had given tickets. In the outer balcony there were three tiers deep. The brightness of scarlet-liveried men, the Royal waiters, and every one in full dress made a scene of unparalleled splendour. In front of us there stood a temporary wooden stable, in which for many days had lived the horse of the Champion, with two others, who had been training to perform their difficult task of backing down the whole length of Westminster Hall, (which feat is performed at the close of the feast) when the champion has advanced and thrown down his gauntlet challenge and retires gold goblet in hand . . . to drink the King's health.

"The horse had his last practice early that morning, so we had the sight as far as from the stable to the Hall and back. 'Dymock' was the Champion, an hereditary honour. . . . The Marquis of Anglesea, as Master of the Horse, was one of his escorts. I cannot remember the other, but the Marquis with his cork leg rode the same favourite Arab that carried him at Waterloo (where he lost his leg).

" Another excitement in the early morning was the driving up of Queen Caroline who was in London, and desirous to alarm the King, her husband, and to make a mutiny amongst the soldiers. Terrible were the yells when she appeared, for people were so bent upon their sight-seeing that it was not a favourable moment for her to make an impression. However, she came in her Barouche and four horses and alighted, very near to our house, between the Champion's stable and Mr. Wilde's archway, (at that spot) there was a barrier and a door of fresh deal in it. Up to this door she walked, and from above we could plainly see her, and hear her say aloud, ' Show me to my husband.' Whereupon the large porter in scarlet slammed the door and locked it. A terrible moment to everybody. We children received a strong impression from all that was said by our grown-up neighbours. Yells and a few cheers filled the air : rebellion and confusion were expected. The Queen then crossed the platform that was prepared for the procession. During her absence from the carriage a group of Life Guards surrounded it, and turned the horses' heads, no notice being taken of her. She returned to her carriage pretty much guided to it by the Life Guards, and when she was

WESTMINSTER HALL AND COFFEE HOUSES

From a drawing by Thomas Sandby, R.A.

seated they gathered closely round, and guided the route. I believe that she went to the door of Westminster Abbey, Lord Hood being her escort, and there she tried for admittance, presenting a forged ticket, but she failed in that purpose and drove away altogether from the regal scene.

" The Procession came out from Westminster Hall, beginning with an elderly lady in white satin with a crimson satin hood on her shoulders edged with gold lace, in shape like an M.A. Oxford hood ; and bearing a golden basket from which she strewed flowers. She was the Royal Flower Girl, Miss Fellows, and was followed by eight assistants walking two and two, all beautiful and of high birth, carrying larger baskets between them, and strewing flowers ; their white dresses looped with white roses.

" Then came the long line of wonderfully bright figures increasing in dignity till Dukes and Royal Dukes came next to the King, over whose head was borne a canopy of cloth of gold on ivory staves. He, poor man, seemed almost lifeless—large and heavy, with large pallid cheeks and wearing a large crown-like cap of velvet and ermine. His train extended far, borne by eight young pages, all sons of Dukes. All walked with heads uncovered, but on the return, (when) the King wore his crown, all the Peers wore their coronets. Two figures were very prominent,

H

CHAPTER XIII

A NEW HOME IN WESTMINSTER

MRS. LEFROY writes : " I seem to enter a new epoch of my young life after the coronation of George IV, and our establishment in the larger house in Palace Yard, the red brick house, once the Official residence of Horace Walpole when he was Chancellor of the Exchequer. Papa," she adds, "became 1st Clerk Assistant (in 1821) instead of 2nd and succeeded to this house which was situated facing the river, but beyond the Speaker's house and adjoining the House of Lords. It was in a line with Westminster Hall, and to the right stood the old Star Chamber of Queen Elizabeth's date. The house was entered by a long passage passing the cellar door where Guy Fawkes was once busy with his barrels."

Whilst Rickman held the post of 2nd Clerk Assistant his salary had been £1500, but on his translation to that of Clerk Assistant it became £2500. The character of his work changed a good deal and he was in a position in which he could suggest and

SOMERSET HOUSE AND "STAIRS"

carry forward several useful measures respecting a change in the procedure of the House. His capacity for work was extraordinary, for in spite of his heavy official duties, he found time, we are told, to help many a friend with his knowledge of economies. " His letters to Southey, at this period, nearly all contain answers to questions which had arisen in the course of Southey's literary work, in many cases filling four or five closely written folio pages." *

To return to Mrs. Lefroy. " We could see," she writes, " from our windows in the new house across the foot of old Westminster bridge, which by the way (my father) said would be shaken to its foundations when old London bridge was taken down. It fulfilled his prediction and became unsafe, being built in pontoons (I think is the term), *i.e.* each pier cased in a sunken boat. The tide becoming more rapid after the solid dam of London bridge was gone, it undermined these boats and shook the piers.

" It was a favourite pastime to hire a wherry for an hour with a waterman to row. He wore a heavy jacket crimson or blue with full frill at the waist and a metal badge on his breast and his number. In this way we went usually to the Annual Exhibition of the Royal Academy Pictures then shown at Somerset House and landed at the Water Gate entrance under the deep stone arch.

* See *Life of John Rickman*, by Orlo Williams.

"Sometimes we went to Vauxhall Gardens—this was an evening promenade, becoming rather vulgar—but it had its day of fashion. The singers were Braham and Catalini, very famous in their day. It ended with a grand display of fireworks at midnight when Madame Sacchi ran up a tight rope, as it seemed, into the flames.

"There was also Astley's Theatre across the water where once a year we went to see the horses, by dint of asking leave of Papa in a Latin letter."

There is a curious little volume in our possession entitled :

" Plan

of the

T H A M E S,

with its

Bridges & Stairs

from Battersea Bridge

to Greenwich."

It is dated 1829. We hope to reproduce it in this book.

"I should mention what I remember of our Sundays and the Church of St. Margaret's where we went every Sunday morning. Papa had an Official seat in the gallery next to the Speaker at the west end of

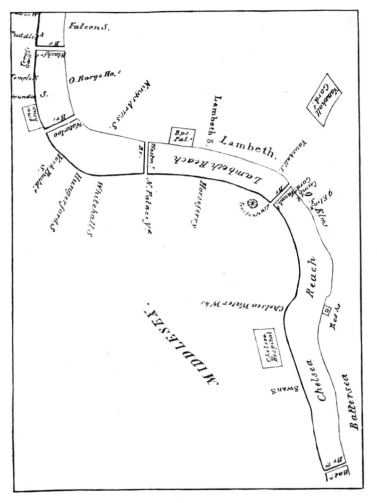

PART OF AN OLD PLAN OF THE THAMES SHEWING THE BRIDGES AND "STAIRS" FROM THE TEMPLE TO BATTERSEA

the Church, where there were crimson silk curtains surrounding their large square pew with the Lion and Unicorn in plaster relief, but from Official dignity in Church our dear Father liked to escape, and so we sat in the side aisle under the gallery and entered at a different door.

" On a State Service day, Ascension, Restoration, &c. the Speaker in his wig and gown comes to Church, the mace being carried before him to the State pew.

" The only clergyman in charge of the large Parish was an aged curate Mr. Groves by name, rather grim and small I remember. He was in some way attached to the Princess Augusta and preached in the morning. There was a Lecturer paid by subscription in the afternoon, a Mr. Stevens, very popular and much liked by Mrs. Abbott. He was made Chaplain to the House of Commons and became afterwards Dean of Rochester."

merriment.   His laugh was seldom excited by jokes
merely ludicrous ; it was never spiteful ; and his
quiet smile was sometimes inexpressibly sweet ;
perhaps it had a touch of sadness in it.   His mouth
was well-shaped ; his lip tremulous with expression ; his brown eyes were quick, restless and
glittering ; and he had a grand head, full of thought."
Leigh Hunt said that " he had a head worthy of
Aristotle."   Hazlitt calls it " a fine Titian head, full
of dumb eloquence."

After alluding to the severe trials that beset his
early life, Barry Cornwall says : " Nevertheless out
of this desert in which no hope was visible, he rose
up eventually a cheerful man (cheerful when his
days were not clouded by his sister's illness) ; a
charming companion, full of pleasant and gentle
fancies, and the ' finest humourist of his age.' "

Speaking of Lamb's friends he says : " Leigh
Hunt from temperament was more alive to pleasant
influences (sunshine, freedom for work, rural walks,
complimentary words) than the others.   Hazlitt
cared little for these things : a fierce argument or
a well-contested game at rackets was more to his
taste : whilst Lamb's pleasures (except perhaps
from his pipe) lay amongst the books of the old
English writers, more especially with men who had
been unjustly forgotten.

" Hazlitt (who was ordinarily very shy) was the

THE STAR CHAMBER IN 1832

From a sketch by Anne Rickman, afterwards Mrs. Lefroy

best talker of the three. Lamb said the most pithy and brilliant things. Hunt displayed the most ingenuity. All three sympathized often with the same persons or the same books ; and this no doubt cemented the intimacy that existed between them for so many years."

Lamb's affection for books of a past time extended even to their faded and dilapidated appearance. " How beautiful to a genuine lover of reading," he remarks in one of the Essays of Elia, " are the sullied leaves and worn-out appearances, nay the very odour (beyond Russia), if we would not forget kind feelings in fastidiousness, of an old *Circulating Library*, *Tom Jones*, or the *Vicar of Wakefield* ! How they speak of the thousand thumbs that have turned over their pages with delight ! . . . Who would have them a whit less soiled ? What better condition could one desire to see them in ? "

In the Essay entitled " Old China " we find this same love of old books again transpires. Now it is his cousin Bridget Elia (*alias* Mary Lamb) who is speaking. " I wish the good old times would come again," she exclaims, " when we were not quite so rich ; I do not want to be poor, but there was a middle state "—so she was pleased to ramble on—" in which I am sure we were a great deal happier." She was fond of dwelling upon their " phantom wealth," as Lamb calls it.

" A purchase is but a purchase now that you have money enough to spare. Formerly it used to be a triumph. . . .

" Do you remember the brown suit, which you made to hang upon you till all your friends cried shame upon you, it grew so threadbare—and all because of that folio *Beaumont and Fletcher* which you dragged home late at night from Barker's in Covent Garden ? Do you remember how we eyed it for weeks before we could make up our minds to the purchase and had not come to a decision till it was near 10 o'clock of the Saturday night when you set off from Islington, fearing you should be too late—and when the old bookseller with some grumbling opened his shop, and by the twinkling taper (for he was setting bedwards) lighted out the relic from his dusty treasures—and when you lugged it home wishing it were twice as cumbersome—and when you presented it to me—and when we were exploring the perfectness of it (*collating* you called it)—and while I was repairing some of the loose leaves with paste, which your impatience would not suffer to be left till daybreak—was there no pleasure in being a poor man ? "

It seems that Lamb had early inspired Barry Cornwall with a love for the great dramatists of Queen Elizabeth's time, " the old masters of humanity," as he calls them. In his Essay " On Books and

Reading " Elia remarks : " Milton almost requires a solemn service of music to be played before you enter upon him. But he brings his music to which who listens had need bring docile thoughts and purged ears.

" Winter evenings—the World shut out—with less of ceremony the gentle Shakespeare enters. At such a season *The Tempest* or his own *Winter's Tale* —These two poets you cannot avoid reading aloud."

Barry Cornwall used to hear Lamb read aloud his own Essays occasionally. He speaks of " his voice so sincere and earnest," and adds : " No one, as I believe, will ever taste the flavour of certain writers as he has done. He was the last true lover of antiquity." And alluding to the Essays of Elia he remarks : " They are natural with a self-pleasing quaintness. The phrases are not affected ; but are derived from our ancestors, now gone to another country, they are brought back from the land of shadows and made denizens of England in modern times."

In the year 1819 Lamb made an offer of marriage to Fanny Kelly, the well-known actress. He had a great admiration for her character both public and private, and much enjoyed her society. But he was grieved to see her forced to work, often under heavy pressure, in order to support a sick mother and an intemperate father, and he longed to bring some relief to her if possible. It seems to us that this was the strongest motive that influenced Lamb in the affair.

Miss Kelly refused the offer at once, in the following letter, dated Henrietta Street, July 20, 1819 :

" An early and deeply rooted attachment has fixed my heart on one from whom no worldly prospect can well induce me to withdraw it, but while I thus *frankly* and decidedly decline your proposal, believe me I am not insensible to the high honour which the preference of such a mind as yours confers upon me—let me, however, hope that all thought upon this subject will end with this letter, and that you will henceforth encourage no other sentiment towards me than esteem of my private character, and a continuance of that approbation of my humble talents which you have already expressed so much and so often to my advantage and gratification."

Thus, we are told, " a single day saw the whole drama played out."

No love passages can ever have passed between the two, considering the circumstances in which Miss Kelly was placed, and the affair seems in no way to have influenced Lamb's life. The abiding influence on his life was his early love for " the fair-haired maid " whose sweet image appears to us in the early poems and in the " Dream Children."

" How his love then prospered," writes his intimate friend Talfourd, " we cannot ascertain, but we know how nobly that love and all hopes of the earthly blessings attendant on such an affection were resigned on the catastrophe which darkened the following year (1796) in the Lambs' household."

" In a series of Essays by Lamb entitled *Popular Fallacies* the last essay is remarkable," writes Barry Cornwall, " for a sentence which seems to refer to Alice W——. ' We were never much in the world,' he says ; ' disappointment early struck a dark veil between us and its dazzling illusions. We once thought life to be something, but it has unaccountably fallen from us before its time.' "

Wordsworth had written *The Excursion* in 1814, which had produced a tempest of adverse criticism led on by the celebrated article in the *Edinburgh Review*, beginning with the words, " This will never do." Lamb had a great admiration for Wordsworth, and he wrote an article in defence of the poem that appeared in the *Quarterly Review*, but it was so terribly curtailed and mangled by the Editor—his warm expressions being changed to cold ones and the whole purport of the review reversed—that in Lamb's phrase " the eyes were pulled out and the bleeding sockets left." Under such conditions Lamb begged Wordsworth not to read the article.

Soon after Talfourd had made the acquaintance of Lamb he writes : " The next time I saw him he came almost breathless into the Office and proposed to give me what I should have chosen as the greatest of all possible honours and delight—an introduction to Wordsworth, who I learned with a palpitating heart was actually at the next door.   I hurried out with my kind conductor, and a minute after was presented by Lamb to the person whom in all the world I venerated most with this preface : ' Wordsworth, give me leave to introduce to you my only admirer.' "

" I have a vivid recollection of Wordsworth," writes Barry Cornwall, " who was a very grave man, with strong features and a deep voice.   I met him first at the Chambers (they were in the Temple) of Mr. Henry Crabb Robinson, one of the most amiable of men.   I was a young versifier, and Wordsworth was just emerging out of a cloud of ignorant contumely into the sunrise of his fame.   He was fond (perhaps too fond) of reciting his own poetry, before friends and strangers.   I was not attracted by his manner, which was almost too solemn, but I was deeply impressed by some of the weighty notes in his voice when he was delivering one of his oracles.   I forget whether it was *Dion* or the beautiful poem of *Laodamia* that he read ; but I remembered the reading long afterwards, as one recollects the roll of the spent thunder. . . ."

Hazlitt has thus described his face : " There was a severe worn pressure of thoughts about his temples, a fire in his eyes (as if he saw something in objects

DOORWAY OF SHELLEY'S HOUSE
17 Great College Street

more than the outward appearance), an intense narrow forehead, a Roman nose and cheeks furrowed by strong purpose and feeling." After hearing him read aloud the story of *Peter Bell* in the open air amidst his own mountains, Hazlitt remarks : " Whatever be thought of the poem, his face was a book where men might read strange matters, and he announced the fate of his hero in prophetic tones."

We learn, however, from Hazlitt, that notwithstanding his constitutional gravity, Wordsworth's face sometimes revealed indications of dry humour.

Wordsworth often visited Lamb in his Chambers when in town. Crabb Robinson writes in his Diary in June 1820 : " At nine went to Lamb's where Mr. and Mrs. Wordsworth were. . . . Lamb read some recent compositions which Wordsworth cordially praised ; he seemed to enjoy Lamb's society. Not much was said about (Wordsworth's) new volume of poems. But he himself spoke of his *Brownie's Cell* as his favourite."

The painter Haydon has given us a graphic description of a gathering at his house of some of the leading writers of the day, among whom were Wordsworth, Lamb and Keats.

Writing in 1817 he says : " On December 28th the immortal dinner came off in my Painting-room—with Jerusalem towering up behind us as a background. Wordsworth was in fine cue and we had a glorious

I

set to—on Homer, Shakespeare, Milton and Virgil; Lamb got exceedingly merry and exquisitely witty, and his fun in the midst of Wordsworth's solemn intonations of oratory was like the sarcasm and wit of the fool in the intervals of Lear's passion.

" He then in a strain of humour beyond description abused me for putting Newton's head into my picture—' a fellow,' said he, ' who believed nothing unless it was as clear as the three sides of a triangle ! ' And then he and Keats agreed he had destroyed all the poetry of the rainbow by reducing it to the prismatic colours. It was impossible to resist him, and we all drank Newton's health and confusion to mathematics. It was delightful to see the good humour of Wordsworth in giving in to all our frolics without affectation and laughing as merrily as the best of us."

Talfourd, who was one of the guests, says : " It was indeed an immortal evening. Wordsworth's fine intonation as he quoted Milton and Virgil, Keats's eager inspired look, Lamb's quaint sparkle of lambent humour, so speeded the stream of conversation, that in my life I never passed a more delightful time."

Lamb and Keats seldom met, but Lamb greatly admired Keats's poetry, as is shown by his review of *St. Agnes Eve* in the *New Times* and by his statement to Crabb Robinson that he thought it next to Wordsworth.

S. T. COLERIDGE
By Northcote

Shelley's poetry did not appeal specially to Lamb, but Shelley, on the other hand, admired Lamb deeply. He wrote to Leigh Hunt in 1819 : " What a lovely thing is his *Rosamund Gray*! How much knowledge of the sweetest and deepest parts of our nature in it ! When I think of such a mind as Lamb's —when I see how unnoticed remain things of such exquisite and complete perfection—what should I hope for myself, if I had not higher objects in view than fame ! " a criticism that pleased Lamb when Hunt repeated it to him.

Coleridge has been styled " the great friend and mentor of Charles Lamb's youth." They had been schoolfellows together at Christ's Hospital, and there was a strong tie of friendship between them. Barry Cornwall when writing of them observes : " The two friends were very dissimilar—the one wandering amongst lofty ill-defined objects whilst the other clung to the realities of life." Coleridge's theories, inspired largely, no doubt, by the study of German metaphysics, were too vast and unreal to take hold of an audience, but those, we are told, who had ever heard his noble outpourings of high ideals, delivered in a voice " musical as Apollo's lute " which rose from the gentlest pitch of conversation to the height of impassioned eloquence, could never forget it.

Hazlitt was staying at one time in the beautiful country around Nether Stowey in Somersetshire in company with both Wordsworth and Coleridge. One day Wordsworth, looking out of the low latticed window of their cottage, said : " How beautifully the sun sets on that yellow bank ! "   " I thought within myself," says Hazlitt, " with what eyes these poets see nature ! and ever after when I saw the sunset stream upon the objects facing it, conceived I had made a discovery or thanked Mr. Wordsworth for having made one for me. Coleridge has told me," he remarks, " that he liked to compose in walking over uneven ground, or breaking through the straggling branches of a copsewood ; whereas Wordsworth always wrote (if he could) walking up and down a straight gravel walk, or in some spot where the continuity of his verse met with no collateral interruption. I (afterwards) got into a metaphysical argument with Wordsworth while Coleridge was explaining the different notes of the nightingale to his sister in which we neither of us succeeded in making ourselves perfectly clear or intelligible."

Hazlitt tells us that on one occasion Coleridge, having been present at a big dinner in Birmingham, returned to smoke his pipe in peace in an adjoining room, where he unwittingly fell fast asleep on a sofa ! " There the company found him to their no small surprise, which was increased to wonder when he started up of a sudden and, rubbing his eyes, looked about him and launched into a three-hour description of the third heaven of which he had had a dream."

A visit to Coleridge was looked upon by Lamb as affording a means of giving a rare treat to those who could appreciate it. " I well remember," writes Talfourd, " the flush of prideful pleasure which came over his face as he would hurry on his way to the India House, into the Office in which I was a pupil, and stammer out the welcome invitation for the evening."

When Coleridge took his seat in the familiar gathering " the genial hubbub of voices was still, critics, philosophers and poets were contented to listen and toil-worn lawyers' clerks from the India House and members of the Stock Exchange grew romantic while he spoke. His benignity of manner placed his auditors entirely at their ease, and inclined them to listen delighted to the sweet, low tone in which he began to discourse on some high theme . . . his hearers were unable to grasp his theories, which were indeed too vast to be exhibited in the longest conversation ; but they perceived noble images, generous suggestions, affecting pictures of virtue, which enriched their minds and nurtured their best affections.

" Coleridge was sometimes induced to recite portions of *Christabel*, then enshrined in manuscript from eyes profane, and gave a bewitching effect to its wizard lines."

CHAPTER XV

THE WORLD BEHIND THE CURTAIN

HAPPILY for us the lives of both Charles Lamb and William Hazlitt overlapped the period of some of the great actors of the late eighteenth century ; so we have the inestimable advantage of their stirring accounts of these actors as eye-witnesses.

" Who shall give us Mrs. Siddons again," exclaims Hazlitt, " but in a waking dream, a beatific vision of past years ? Who shall in our time—or even to the eye of fancy—fill the stage like her with the dignity of their persons and the emanations of their minds ? Who shall stalk over the stage of horror, its presiding genius, or ' play the hostess ' at the banqueting scene of murder ? . . . She was tragedy personified. . . . She embodied, to our imagination, the fables of mythology, of the heroic and deified mortals of elder time. She was not only the idol of the people, she not only hushed the tumult of the pit in breathless expectation . . . but to the retired and lonely

student," adds Hazlitt, "through long years of solitude, her face shone as if an eye had appeared from
heaven ; her name has been as if a voice had opened
the chambers of the human heart, or as if a trumpet
had awakened the sleeping and the dead.

" (But yet) her nature seemed always above the
circumstances with which she had to struggle, her
soul to be greater than the passion labouring in her
breast.   Grandeur was the cradle in which her genius
was rocked ; for her *to be* was to be sublime.   The
least word she uttered seemed to float to the end of
the stage, the least motion of her hand seemed to
command awe and obedience."

We have the testimony of the moving power of
Mrs. Siddons's voice given by another contemporary
—that of a young girl who wrote in after life : " There
is no giving an adequate impression of the might,
the majesty, and grace she possessed, nor of the
effect on a young heart of the deep and mysterious
tones of her voice." *

Hazlitt did not live early enough to see Garrick
act, but he has recorded some striking instances of
the effect of Garrick's marvellous powers upon an
audience.   " I have heard," he writes, " that once
when Garrick was acting Lear, the spectators in the
front row of the pit, not being able to see him well
in the kneeling scene, when he utters the curse, rose

* See *Remains of Mrs. Richard French.*

up, when those behind them rose up too, and in this manner the whole pit rose up without uttering a syllable, and so that you might hear a pin drop. (Once) the crown of straw which he wore, fell off or was discomposed, which would have produced a burst of laughter at any common actor to whom such an accident had happened ; but such was the deep interest in the character, and such the power of rivetting the attention possessed by this actor, that not the slightest notice was taken of the circumstance, but the whole audience remained bathed in silent tears.".

Charles Lamb writes in one of the Essays of Elia : " The casual sight of an old Play Bill which I picked up the other day—I know not by what chance it was preserved so long—tempts me to call to mind a few of the Players, who make the principal figure in it. It presents the cast of parts in the *Twelfth Night*, at the old Drury Lane Theatre two-and-thirty years ago. There is something very touching in these old remembrances. . . . ' Orsino, by Mr. Barrymore.' What a full Shakespearian sound it carries ! How fresh to memory arise the image and the manner of the gentle actor !

" Those who have only seen Mrs. Jordan within the last ten or fifteen years can have no adequate notion of her performance of such parts as Ophelia,

OLD WESTMINSTER BRIDGE

From a sketch by **Anne Rickman**, *afterwards Mrs. Lefroy*

Helena, in *All's Well that Ends Well*, and Viola. Her voice has latterly acquired a coarseness which suited well enough with her Nells and Hoydens, but in those days it sank, with her steady, melting eye, into the heart. . . . There is no giving an account how she delivered the disguised story of her love for Orsino . . . but when she had declared her sister's history to be a ' blank ' and that she ' never told her love,' there was a pause, as if the story had ended— and then the image of the ' worm in the bud ' came up as a new suggestion—and the heightened image of ' Patience ' still followed after that as by some growing (and not mechanical) process, thought springing up after thought, I would almost say, as they were watered by her tears.

" . . . Mrs. Powel, then in the pride of her beauty, made an admirable Olivia. She was particularly excellent in her unbending scenes in conversation with the Clown. I have seen some Olivias . . . who in these interlocutions have seemed to set their wits at the jester, and to vie conceits with him in downright emulation. But she used him for her sport, like what he was, to trifle a leisure sentence or two with, and then to be dismissed, and she to be the Great Lady still. She touched the imperious fantastic humour of the character with nicety. Her fine spacious person filled the scene.

" The part of Malvolio in the *Twelfth Night* was

performed by Bensley with a richness and a dignity of which the very tradition must be worn out from the stage. . . . Of all the actors who flourished in my time . . . Bensley had most of the swell of soul, was the greatest in the delivery of heroic conceptions. . . . He had the true poetical enthusiasm—the rarest faculty among players. . . . He seized the moment of passion with greatest truth ; like a faithful clock, never striking before the time ; never anticipating or leading you to anticipate. He was totally destitute of trick and artifice. . . . He would have scorned to mountebank it ; and betrayed none of that *cleverness* which is the bane of all serious acting. For this reason, his Iago was the only endurable one which I remember to have seen. No spectator, from his action, could divine more of his artifice than Othello was supposed to do. His confessions in soliloquy alone put you in possession of the mystery. There were no by-intimations to make the audience fancy their own discernment so much greater than that of the Moor—who commonly stands like a great helpless mark, set up for mine Ancient, and a quantity of barren spectators, to shoot their bolts at. The Iago of Bensley did not go to work so grossly. There was a triumphant tone about the character natural to a general consciousness of power. . . . It was not a man setting his wits at a child, and winking all the while at other children, who are mightily pleased at being let into the secret ; but a consummate villain entrapping a noble nature into toils against which no discernment was available, where the manner was as fathomless as the purpose seemed dark, and without motive."

Then, returning to the performance of *Twelfth Night*, Lamb remarks : " There was good foolery too. Few now remember Dodd. What an Aguecheek the stage lost in him ! In expressing slowness of apprehension this actor surpassed all others. . . . He seemed to keep back his intellect, as some have had the power to retard their pulsation. . . . A glimmer of understanding would appear in a corner of his eye, and for lack of fuel go out again.

" If few can remember Dodd, many yet living will not easily forget the pleasant creature who in those days enacted the part of the Clown to Dodd's Sir Andrew—Richard, or rather Dicky Suett—for so in his life-time he delighted to be called. . . . He was the Robin Goodfellow of the stage. . . . Care, that troubles all the world, was forgotten in his composition. Had he had but two grains (nay, half a grain) of it he could never have supported himself upon those two spider's strings which served him as legs. . . . But on he went, scrambling upon these airy stilts of his, with Robin Goodfellow ' thorough brake, thorough briar,' reckless of a scratched face or a torn doublet.

" Shakespeare foresaw him when he framed his fools and jesters.   They have all the true Suett stamp, a loose and shambling gait, a slippery tongue . . . ; in words light as air venting truths deep as the centre ; with idlest rhymes tagging conceit when busiest, singing with Lear in the tempest, or Sir Toby at the buttery-hatch."

At the period of which we are writing Madame Pasta and Mademoiselle Mars were conspicuous figures on the London Boards, and Hazlitt has left us an interesting comparison of the respective powers of the two actors.

" I liked Mademoiselle Mars exceedingly well," he writes, " till I saw Madame Pasta, whom I liked so much better.   The reason is, the one is the perfection of French, the other of natural acting. Madame Pasta is Italian, and she might be English— Mademoiselle Mars belongs emphatically to her Country ; the scene of her triumphs is Paris.   She plays naturally too, but it is French nature.   Let me explain.   She has, it is true, none of the vices of the French Theatre, its extravagance, its grimaces and affectation, but she seems to put an artificial restraint upon herself. . . . When she enters, she advances in a straight line from the other end to the middle of the stage, with the slight unvarying trip of her country-women, and then stops short as if under the drill of a *fugle-man*. . . . Her acting is an inimitable study or consummate rehearsal of the part as a preparatory performance ; she hardly yet appears to have assumed the character ; something more is wanting, and that something you find in Madame Pasta. If Mademoiselle Mars has to smile, a slight and evanescent expression of pleasure passes across the surface of her face ; . . . when Madame Pasta smiles, a beam of joy seems to have struck upon her heart, and to irradiate her countenance. Her whole face is bathed and melted in expression. . . . When she speaks it is in music. When she moves it is without thinking whether she is graceful or not. In acting the part of Nina—a love-sick damsel—Madame Pasta thinks no more of the audience than Nina herself could, if she could be observed by stealth. When she walks in upon the stage and looks about her with the same unconsciousness or timid wonder of the young stag in the forest ; when she moves her limbs as carelessly as a tree its branches ; when she unfolds one of her divine expressions of countenance, which reflect the inmost feelings of the soul, as the calm deep lake reflects the face of heaven ; . . . she gives up herself entirely to the impression of the part . . . . and is transformed into the very being she represents. She does not act the character of Nina—she is it, looks it, breathes it . . . as if she were really a love-sick, care-crazed maiden, occupied with one deep sorrow, and who had no other idea or interest in the world.   This alone is true nature and true art."

Liston and Munden were the greatest comic actors of our period.   Lamb has devoted one of the Essays of Elia to the " Acting of Munden."

" Not many nights ago," he writes, " I had come home from seeing this extraordinary performer in '*Cockletop*' ; and when I retired to my pillow, his whimsical image still stuck by me, in a manner to threaten sleep.   In vain I tried to divest myself of it, by conjuring up the most opposite associations. . . . But I was not to escape so easily.   No sooner did I fall into slumbers, than the same image, only more perplexing, assailed me in the shape of dreams. Not one Munden, but five hundred, were dancing before me. . . . O for the power of the pencil to have fixed them when I awoke !

" There is one face of Farley, one face of Knight, one (but what a one it is !) of Liston ; but Munden has none that you can properly pin down and call his.   When you think he has exhausted his battery of looks, in unaccountable warfare with your gravity, suddenly he sprouts out an entirely new set of features, like Hydra.   He is not one, but legion. . . . Out of some invisible wardrobe he dips for faces, as his friend Suett used to do for wigs, and fetches them out as easily. . . .

" I have seen this gifted actor in Sir Christopher
Curry—in *Old Dornton*—diffuse a glow of sentiment
which has made the pulse of a crowded theatre beat
like that of one man ; when he has come in aid of
the pulpit, doing good to the moral heart of a people.
I have seen some faint approaches to this sort of
excellence in other players. But in the grand
grotesque of farce, Munden stands out as single and
unaccompanied as Hogarth. Hogarth, strange to
tell, had no followers. The school of Munden began,
and must end, with himself.

" Who like him," continues Lamb, " can throw,
or ever attempted to throw, a preternatural interest
over the commonest daily-life objects ? A table or
a joint-stool, in his conception, rises into a dignity
equivalent to Cassiopeia's chair. . . . You could not
speak of it with more deference, if it were mounted
into the firmament. ' A beggar in the hands of
Michael Angelo,' says Fuseli, ' rose the Patriarch of
Poverty.' So the gusto of Munden antiquates and
ennobles what it touches."

Talfourd tells us that " in the year 1824 Munden
quitted the stage in the mellowness of his powers. . . .
On the last night of his appearance, Lamb was very
desirous to attend, but every place in the boxes had
long since been secured and he was not strong enough
to stand the rush of the crowd in order to attain a
place in the pit. Munden, however, anticipated his

wish by providing for him and Miss Lamb places in a corner of the orchestra, close to the stage. The first play had concluded, and the audience were impatiently waiting for the farce in which the great comedian was to delight them for the last time, when my attention," remarks Talfourd, " was suddenly called to Lamb by Miss Kelly, who sat with my party in one of the upper boxes, but overlooking the radiant hollow below us to our friend. In his hand, directly beneath the line of stage-lights, glistened a huge porter-pot which he was draining; while the broad face of old Munden was seen thrust out from the door by which the musicians enter, watching the close of the draught when he might receive and hide the portentous beaker from the gaze of the admiring neighbours. Some unknown benefactor had sent four pots of stout to keep up the veteran's heart during his last trial; and not able to drink them all, he bethought him of Lamb, and without considering the wonder that would be excited in the brilliant crowd who surrounded him, conveyed himself the cordial chalice to Lamb's parched lips."

Liston stood very high as a comedian of the humorous type, but he did not deal in the extreme of farce. Barry Cornwall, writing of the two actors, says : " Munden had faces innumerable ; Liston had only one, but what a face ! " he adds, as Lamb had done, admitting it to be beyond all vain description.

Perhaps this subject of universal laughter and admiration never received such a compliment ; except from Hazlitt, who after commenting on Hogarth's excellence, his invention, his character, his satire, etc., concludes by saying : " I have never seen anything in the expression of comic humour equal to Hogarth's humour except Liston's face."

One of Liston's most celebrated characters was that of Paul Pry, and the tradition has come down to us from a contemporary, that he used to make his entrance upon the stage, surreptitiously as it were, and peeping first through a half-open doorway with an inquisitive look upon the company assembled would remark, " I hope I don't intrude."

Kemble took his leave of the stage on Monday night, June 25, 1817, in the character of Coriolanus. " . . . It is near twenty years since we first saw him in the same character," writes Hazlitt, " yet how short the interval seems ! . . . We forget numberless things that have happened to ourselves . . . but not the first time of our seeing Mr. Kemble, nor shall we easily forget the last.

" Coriolanus was one of the first in which we remember to have seen him ; and it was one in which we were not sorry to part with him, for we wished to see him appear like himself to the last. There was no abatement of spirit and energy and none of grace

K

and dignity ; his look, his action, his expression of the character were the same as they ever were, they could not be finer.

" It has always appeared to us that the range of characters in which Mr. Kemble more particularly shone, and was superior to every other actor, were those which consisted in the development of some one solitary sentiment or exclusive passion. From a want of rapidity, of scope and variety he was often deficient in expressing the bustle and complication of different interests, nor did he possess the faculty of overpowering the mind by sudden and irresistible bursts of passion. In Leontes in the *Winter's Tale* (a character he at one time played often), the growing jealousy of the King, and the exclusive possession which this passion gradually obtains over his mind, were marked by him in the finest manner, particularly where he exclaims :

> . . . Is whispering nothing ?
> Is leaning cheek to cheek ?   Is meeting noses ?
> Kissing with inside lip ?   Stopping the career
> Of laughter with a sigh ?—a note infallible
> Of braking honesty ;—horsing foot on foot ?
> Skulking in corners ?   Wishing clocks more swift ?
> Hours, minutes ? . . . Is this nothing ?
> Why, then the world and all that's in't is nothing ;
> The covering sky is nothing ; Bohemia's nothing ;
> My wife is nothing ; if this be nothing.

" In the course of this enumeration every proof told stronger and followed with quicker and harder

strokes, his conviction became more rivetted at every
step of his progress, and at the end, his mind and
' every corporal agent' appeared wound up to a
frenzy of despair. . . .

"In Hamlet, on the contrary, Mr. Kemble, in
our judgment, unavoidably failed from a want of
flexibility, of that quick sensibility which yields to
every motive, and is borne away with every breath
of fancy, which is distracted in the multiplicity of its
reflections, and lost in the uncertainty of its resolu-
tions. There is a perpetual undulation of feeling
in the character of Hamlet; but in Mr. Kemble's
acting ' there was neither variableness nor shadow
of turning.' He played it like a man in armour,
with a determined inveteracy of purpose, in one
undeviating straight line, which is as remote from
the natural grace and indolent susceptibility of the
character as the sharp angles and abrupt starts to
produce an effect which Mr. Kean throws into it."

After seeing Kean perform the character of Lear,
Hazlitt writes : " We need not say how much our
expectations have been previously excited to see
Mr. Kean in the character of Lear, and we are sorry
to be obliged to add that they were very considerably
disappointed. We had hoped to witness something
of the same effect produced upon an audience that
Garrick is reputed to have done in the part which
made Dr. Johnson resolve never to see him repeat

it — the impression was so terrific and over-whelming."

Lear was Kean's favourite part, " but the impression made on our minds was that instead of its being his master-piece he was to seek in many parts of the character ;—that the general conception was often perverse and feeble, and there were only two or three places where he could be said to electrify the house. It is altogether inferior to his Othello. . . . Into the bursts and starts and torrent of the passion of Othello this excellent actor appeared to have flung himself completely . . . but there is something (we don't know how) in the gigantic outspread sorrows of Lear that seems to elude his grasp and baffle his attempts at comprehension. The passion in Othello pours along, so to speak, like a river, torments itself in restless eddies, or is hurled from its dizzy height, like a sounding cataract. That in Lear is more like a sea, swelling, chafing, raging without bound, without hope, without beacon or anchor. Torn from the hold of his affections and fixed purposes, he floats, a mighty wreck, in the wide world of sorrows. . . . We had thought that Mr. Kean would take possession of this time-worn venerable figure, ' that has out-lasted a thousand storms, a thousand winters ' . . . that he would set up a living copy of it on the stage ; but he failed . . . perhaps the genius of no living actor can be expected to cope with Lear."

Pope said of Garrick in the earlier part of his career : " That young man never had his equal and will never have a rival." It seems to us that the century and a half and more that have passed since that prophecy was made have amply proved its truth.

CHAPTER XVI

QUIPS AND CRANKS

IT was in the year 1822 that Lamb first made the acquaintance of Tom Hood, then a young man of twenty-three, who was assisting the Editor of the *London Magazine* in his literary work. Hood had the warmest admiration for Lamb, and Lamb, we are told, " had as kindly a feeling for Hood as for any of the younger writers, while his talent amazed him. ' That half Hogarth,' he once called him."

Hood has recorded his reminiscences of Lamb in *Hood's Own*. Here is an account of their first meeting : " I was sitting one morning," he writes, " beside our Editor busily correcting proofs, when a visitor was announced whose name grumbled in a low voice . . . did not resound distinctly on my tympanum. However, the door opened, and in came a stranger—a figure remarkable at a glance, with a fine head on a small spare body, supported by two almost immaterial legs. He was clothed in sables of a by-gone fashion, but there was something present about him that certified he was neither a divine nor a physician, nor a schoolmaster. From a certain neatness and sobriety in his dress coupled with his sedate bearing he might have been taken . . . for a Quaker in black. He looked still more like (what he really was) a literally Modern Antique or New-Old author, a living Anachronism, contemporary at once with Burton the elder and Colman the younger. Meanwhile he advanced with rather a peculiar gait . . . and with a cheerful ' How d'ye do ? ' and one of the blandest, sweetest smiles that ever brightened a manly countenance, held out two fingers to the Editor.

" The two gentlemen in black soon fell into discourse ; and whilst they conferred the Lavater principle within me set to work upon the interesting specimen thus presented to its speculations. It was a striking intellectual face full of wiry lines, physiognomical quips and cranks, that gave it great character. There was much earnestness about the brows and a deal of speculation in the eyes which were brown and bright and ' quick in turning,' the nose a decided one of no established order ; and there was a handsome smartness about the mouth. Altogether it was no common face—none of those *willow-pattern* ones which Nature turns out by thousands at her potteries. . . . No one who had once seen it could pretend not to know it again. . . . In short, his

face was as original as his figure ; his figure as his
character ; his character as his writings ; his writings
the most original of the age.

" After the literary business had been settled the
Editor invited his contributor to dinner, adding, ' we
shall have a hare,' (when the contributor remarked)
' and—and—and—and many friends.' "

" Lamb," Hood adds, " was shy like myself with
strangers, so that despite my yearnings our first
meeting scarcely amounted to an introduction.   We
were both at dinner amongst the hare's many friends,
but our acquaintance got no further, in spite of a
desperate attempt on my part to attract his notice.
. . .   I had given up all hope when one night,
sitting sick and sad in my bedroom racked with the
rheumatism, the door was suddenly opened, the well-
known quaint figure in black walked in without any
formality, and with a cheerful ' Well, boy, how are
you ? ' and the bland sweet smile, extended the two
fingers.   They were eagerly clutched of course, and
from that hour we were firm friends."

In Talfourd's *Memoirs of Charles Lamb* we find
the following passage given in a footnote :

" An American lady, Mrs. Balmanno, describes a
dinner at the Hoods' at which the Lambs were present.
Lamb, the lady noted, was always playing pranks on
his sister, who was dressed with a quaker-like simplicity in a dove-coloured silk with a transparent ker-

chief of snow-white muslin folded across her bosom. Her behaviour towards him was as of ' some adoring disciple,' her eyes being always fixed on his face ; even when he was talking at the other end of the room she would supply some word that he wanted. On this occasion he was in high spirits, sauntering about the room, his hands behind his back, conversing (with friends) by fits and starts." Mr. Procter quotes the American, N. P. Willis's account of his meeting with Charles and Mary Lamb. " He had been invited by a gentleman in the Temple, Mr. R—— (Robinson ?), to meet Charles Lamb and his sister at breakfast. The Lambs lived at that time a little out of London and were not quite punctual. At last they enter, the gentleman in black small clothes and gaiters, short and very slight in person ; his head set on his shoulders with a thoughtful forward bent, his hair just sprinkled with grey, a beautiful deep-set eye, an aquiline nose and a very indescribable mouth. Whether it expressed most humour or feeling, good-nature or a kind of whimsical peevishness, or twenty other things which passed over it by turns, I cannot in the least be certain! The guest places a large armchair for Mary Lamb ; Charles pulls it away, saying gravely, ' Mary, don't take it ; it looks as if you were going to have a tooth drawn.' "

" Willis told Lamb that he had bought a copy of the *Elia* in America in order to give it to a friend.

'What did you pay for it?' asked Lamb. 'About seven and sixpence.' 'Permit me to pay you that,' said Lamb, counting out the money, with earnestness, on the table. 'I never yet wrote anything that could sell! I am the publisher's ruin. My last poem won't sell—not a copy. Have you seen it?' No, Willis had not. 'It's only eighteenpence and I'll give you sixpence towards it,' said Lamb; and he described where Willis could find it; sticking up in a shop window in the Strand!"

Lamb's love of London is well known, but he could appreciate the beauties of the country also. Barry Cornwall writes: "After his only visit to the Lake country, and beholding Skiddaw, he writes back to his host (Coleridge): 'Oh! its fine black head, and the bleak air at the top of it, with a prospect of mountains all about making you giddy. It was a day that will stand out like a mountain in my life,' adding, however, 'Fleet Street and the Strand are better places to live in, for good and all. I could not live on Skiddaw. I could spend there two or three years; but I must have a prospect of seeing Fleet Street at the end of that time, or I should mope and pine away.'"

In a letter to Wordsworth he had enumerated the objects that he liked so much in London: "These things," he writes, "work themselves into my mind; the room where I was born; a bookcase that has

FLEET STREET

From the old Copperplate Magazine

followed me about like a faithful dog (only exceeding him in knowledge) wherever I have moved, old chairs ; old tables ; squares where I have sunned myself, my old school—these are my mistresses. Have I not enough without your mountains ? "

And then, his thoughts turning to the Temple, he speaks of its quiet, its ample squares and green recesses where the old Dial, " the garden god of Christian gardens," then told of Time, and where " the still living fountain sends up its song into the listening air."

That Lamb felt bitterly his East India bondage is shown abundantly in his letters, " that drudgery of the desk's dead wood," as he styles it ; but he could make fun of his woes. After a brief visit to the country he writes to a fellow-clerk : " Heigh Ho ! Lord have mercy upon me, how many does two and two make ? I am afraid I shall make a poor clerk in future. I am spoiled with rambling among hay-cocks and cows and pigs.

" Adieu ! ye fields, ye shepherds and herdesses, and dairies and cream pots and fairies and dances upon the green.

" I come, I come. Don't drag me so hard by the hair of my head, Genius of British India ! I know my hour is come. Faustus must give up his soul, O Lucifer, O Mephistopheles ! " *

* See *Life of Charles Lamb*, by E. V. Lucas.

But happily in his heart, as Talfourd tells us, " there never was wanting a secret consciousness of the benefits which it ensured for him, the precious independence which he won by his hours of toil, and the freedom of his mind to work only ' at his own sweet will,' which his confinement to the desk obtained."

There is an account of an animated discussion held in Lamb's rooms in the Temple one evening that forms the subject of an Essay by Hazlitt entitled " Of Persons one would wish to have seen," the subject being suggested, it seems, by Lamb.

" On the matter being started, A—— said, ' I suppose the two first persons you would choose to see would be the two greatest names in English literature—Sir Isaak Newton and Mr. Locke ? ' In this A——, as usual, reckoned without his host. Everyone burst out laughing at the expression of Lamb's face, on which impatience was restrained by courtesy. ' Yes, the greatest names,' he stammered out hastily, ' but they were not persons—not persons.' ' Not persons,' said A——, looking wise and foolish at the same time, afraid his triumph might be premature. ' That is,' rejoined Lamb, ' not characters you know.'

" Presently A—— remarked : ' I shall guess no more—who is it then you would like to see " in his habit as he lived " if you had your choice of the whole

range of English literature ? ' Lamb then named
Sir Thomas Browne and Fulke Greville, the friend of
Sir Philip Sidney, as the two writers whom he should
feel the greatest pleasure to encounter on the floor of
his apartment in their nightgown and slippers, and
to exchange friendly greeting with them.

"At this A—— laughed outright and conceived
Lamb was jesting with him ; but as no one followed
his example, he thought there might be something
in it and waited for an explanation in a state of
whimsical suspense. Lamb then, as well as I can
remember . . . went on as follows : ' The reason
why I pitch upon these two authors is that their
writings are riddles, and they themselves the most
mysterious of personages. They resemble the sooth-
sayers of old who dealt in dark hints and doubtful
oracles ; and I should like to ask them the meaning
of what no mortal but themselves, I should suppose,
can fathom. . . .' ' I am afraid, in that case,' said
A——, ' that if the mystery were once cleared up the
merit might be lost '—and turning to me whispered
a friendly apprehension that while Lamb continued
to admire these old crabbed authors, he would never
become a popular writer. Dr. Donne was mentioned as a writer of the same period, with a very
interesting countenance whose history was singular,
and whose meaning was often quite as *uncomeatable*
without a personal citation from the dead as that of

any of his contemporaries. The volume was produced ; and while some one was expatiating on the
exquisite simplicity and beauty of the portrait pre-
fixed to the old edition . . .   A—— got hold of the
poetry and exclaiming, ' What have we here ? ' read
the following :

> Here lies a She-Sun, and a He-Moon there,
> She gives the best light to his sphere,
> Or each is both and all, and so
> They unto one another nothing owe.

" There was no resisting this, till Lamb, seizing
the volume, turned to the beautiful ' Lines to his
Mistress dissuading her from accompanying him
abroad,' and read them with suffused features and
a faltering tongue.   Thus the poet writes :

> I'll go and by thy kind leave leave behind
> Thee ! only worthy to nurse it in my mind.
> . . . When I am gone dream me some happiness
> Nor let thy looks our long tried love confess
> . . . Nor in bed fright thy nurse
> With midnight startings crying out Oh, oh,
> Nurse, oh, my love is slain I saw him go
> O'er the white Alps alone ; I saw him I
> Assail'd, fight, taken, stabbed, bleed, fall and die.
> Augur me better chance, except dread Jove,
> Think it enough for me to have had thy love.

" Lamb put it to me if I should like to see Spenser
as well as Chaucer ; and I answered without hesitation, ' No ; for that his beauties were ideal, visionary,
not palpable or personal, and therefore connected
with lesser curiosity about the man.   His poetry was

the essence of romance, a very halo round the bright orb of fancy, and the bringing in the individual might dissolve the charm. No tones of voice could come up to the mellifluous cadence of his verse ; no form but of a winged angel could vie with the airy shapes he has described.'

" Captain Burney muttered something about Columbus, and Martin Burney hinted at the Wandering Jew ; but the last was set aside as spurious, and the first made over to the New World.

" ' I should like,' said Mrs. Reynolds, ' to have seen Pope talking with Patty Blount ; and I *have* seen Goldsmith ! ' Everyone turned round to look at Mrs. Reynolds, as if by doing so they too could get a sight of Goldsmith.

" ' I thought,' said A——, turning short round upon Lamb, ' that you of the Lake School did not like Pope ? ' ' Not like Pope ! My dear Sir, you must be under a mistake—I can read him over and over for ever ! ' . . . Of all persons near our own time Garrick's name was received with the greatest enthusiasm. He presently superseded both Hogarth and Handel, who had been talked of ; but then it was on condition that he should act in tragedy and comedy —in the play and the farce. ' Lear ' and ' Wildair ' and ' Abel Drugger.' What *a sight for sore eyes* that would be ! Who would not part with a year's income at least, almost with a year of his natural life, to be present at it ! ''

CHAPTER XVII

A HOLIDAY HOME

BARRY CORNWALL writes of Lamb : " When my thoughts turn backwards, as they sometimes do, to past days I see my dear old friend again—' in my mind's eye Horatio ' with his outstretched hand and his grave, sweet smile of welcome. It was always in a room of moderate size, comfortably but plainly furnished, that he lived. . . . The only ornaments on his walls were a few engravings in black frames ; one after Leonardo da Vinci ; one after Titian ; and four, I think, by Hogarth, about whom he has written so well. I have heard him express admiration for Leonardo da Vinci that he did not accord to Raffaelle. Raffaelle was too ostentatious of meaning ; his merits were too obvious, too much thrust upon the understanding.

" An old mahogany table was spread out in the middle of the room, round which and near to the walls were old highbacked chairs such as our grandfathers used and a long plain bookcase comfortably filled with old books. These were his ' ragged veterans.' In one of his letters Lamb says, ' My rooms are luxurious, one for prints and one for books. A summer and a winter parlour. . . .' He had not been educated into expensive tastes. His extravagances were confined to books. These were all chosen by himself, all old, and all in ' admired disorder,' yet he could lay his hand on any volume in a moment. ' You never saw,' he writes, ' a bookcase in more true harmony with the contents than what I have nailed up in my room. Though new it has more aptitude for growing old than you shall often see ; as one sometimes gets a friend in the middle of life who becomes an old friend in a short time.'

" Here Charles Lamb sat, when at home, always near the table. At the opposite side was his sister, engaged in some domestic work, knitting or sewing or poring over a modern novel. ' Bridget in some things is behind her years,' says Elia. In fact, although she was ten years older than her brother, she had more sympathy with modern books and with youthful fancies than he had. She wore a neat cap of the fashion of her youth ; an old-fashioned dress. Her face was pale and somewhat square ; but very placid ; with grey intelligent eyes. She was very mild in her way to strangers, and to her brother gentle and tender always. . . . . His affection for her was somewhat less on the surface but always present,

L

and he writes of her as being in a season of distress the truest comforter."

Another contemporary tells us " There was a certain old-world fashion in Mary Lamb's diction, which gave it a most natural and quaintly pleasant effect, and which heightened rather than detracted from the more heartfelt or important things she uttered. She had a way of repeating her brother's words assertingly when he spoke to her. He once said (with his peculiar mood of tenderness beneath blunt abrupt speech) : ' You must die first, Mary.' She nodded with her little quiet and sweet smile : ' Yes, I must die first, Charles.' "

Barry Cornwall in writing of the Essays of Elia says : " In mere variety of subject (extent in a small space) they surpass almost all other essays. They are full of a witty melancholy. Many of them may be termed autobiographical, which trebles their interest with most readers. In them gravity and laughter, fact and fiction are heaped together, leavened in each case by charity and tolerance ; and all are marked by a wise humanity. How he mourns over the ruins of Blakesmoor, once his home in holidays, ' reduced to an antiquity ' ! "

We would fain quote a portion of this beautiful Essay together with another dealing with the same subject, but before doing so would remind the reader how it came to pass that the fine old mansion

of Blakesmoor (really Blakesware) became the holiday
resort of the child Charles Lamb.   It was in this way.
Lamb's mother, we are told, had been a Field,
daughter of a Hertfordshire yeoman.   Her mother,
Mrs. Field, was living, at the time of Lamb's birth, at
Blakesware, near Ware in Hertfordshire, " as house-
keeper and sole custodian of an old mansion belonging to the Plumers."   There her grandchildren often
visited her.

Charles was much attached to his grandmother
and has revived her memory in " Dream Children,"
where he is supposed to be describing her virtues to
her great grandchildren and tells them how good she
was to all her grandchildren, " having us," he adds, " to
the Great House in the holidays, where I, in particular,
used to spend many hours by myself . . . how
I never could be tired with roaming about that
huge mansion with its vast empty rooms, with their
worn-out hangings, fluttering tapestry and carved
oaken panels, with the gilding almost rubbed
out."

Again he writes : " Journeying northward lately
I could not resist going some few miles out of my road
to look upon the remains of the old great house with
which I had been impressed in infancy.   I was
apprised that the owner of it had lately pulled it
down ; still I had a vague notion that it could not all
have perished, that so much solidity with magnifi-

cence could not have been crushed all at once into the mere dust and rubbish which I found it.

" The work of ruin had proceeded with a swift hand indeed, and the demolition of a few weeks had reduced it to—an antiquity.

" I was astonished at the indistinction of everything. Where had stood the great gates ? What bounded the courtyard ? Whereabouts did the outhouses commence ? A few bricks only lay as representatives of that which was so stately and so spacious. Had I seen those brick-and-mortar knaves at their process of destruction, at the plucking of every panel I should have felt the varlets at my heart. I should have cried out to them to spare a plank at least out of the cheerful storeroom, in whose hot window-seat I used to sit and read Cowley, with the grass-plot before me and the hum and flappings of that one solitary wasp, that ever haunted it, about me—it is in mine ears now as oft as summer returns.

" Why, every plank and panel of that house for me had magic in it. I was the true descendant of those old W——s and not the present family of that name who had fled the old waste places. . . .

" Mine—whose else ? thy costly fruit garden with its sun-baked southern wall. . . . I never could be tired with roaming about . . . the spacious old-fashioned gardens which I had almost to myself—or in lying about upon the fresh grass with all the fine

garden smells around me . . . or in watching the
dace that darted to and fro in the fish-pond at the
bottom of the garden, with here and there a great
sulky pike, hanging midway down the water in silent
state as if it mocked at their impertinent friskings."

Returning to the old mansion Elia writes : " Mine,
Blakesmoor, was thy noble marble Hall with the
mosaic pavements and the twelve Cæsars—stately
busts in marble ranged around, of whose counten-
ances, young reader of faces as I was, the frowning
beauty of Nero, I remember, had most of my wonder,
but the mild Galba had my love. There they stood
in the coldness of death but freshness of immortality. . . . The tapestried bedrooms,—tapestry so
much better than painting ; not adorning merely but
peopling the wainscots—at which childhood ever
and anon would steal a look, shifting its coverlet
(replaced as quickly) to exercise its tender courage
in a momentary eye-encounter with those stern bright
visages, staring reciprocally,—all Ovid on the walls in
colours vivider than his descriptions. . . .

" Then that haunted room—in which old Mrs.
Battle died—whereinto I have crept, but always in the
daytime, with a passion of fear ; and a sneaking
curiosity, terror-tainted, to hold communication with
the past.

" It was an old deserted place, yet not so long
deserted but that traces of the splendour of past inmates

were everywhere apparent. The furniture was still standing, even to the tarnished gilt leather battledores and crumbling feathers of shuttlecocks in the nursery, which told that children had once played there. . . . But I was a lonely child and had the range at will of every apartment, knew every nook and corner, wondered and worshipped everywhere."

How little could Mrs. Field have anticipated that the tiny child flitting about the old house and loving its every feature, would in after years, by his great powers as a writer, save it from oblivion!

" The solitude of childhood," writes Elia, " is not so much the mother of thought as it is the feeder of love and silence and admiration. I was here in a lonely temple. Snug firesides—the low-built roof— parlours ten feet by ten—frugal boards and all the homeliness of home—these were the conditions of my birth, the wholesome soil which I was planted in, yet without impeachment to their tenderest lessons, I am not sorry to have had glances of something beyond, and to have taken, if but a peep in childhood, at the contrasting accidents of a great fortune."

We would close this chapter with Lamb's reminiscences of the old family picture gallery; one of whose portraits appealed specially to him. As he roamed along the gallery, giving the ancestors of the Plumers, in fancy, his own family name, " one and then another," he says, " would seem to smile, reaching forward from the canvas to recognize the new relationship—while the others looked grave, as it seemed, at the vacancy in their dwelling, and thoughts of fled posterity.

" That Beauty with the cool, blue pastoral drapery and a lamb—that hung near the great bay window— with the bright yellow Hertfordshire hair and eye of Watchet blue—so like my Alice ! "

Here are some lines by Lamb, describing the charms of " his Alice," that appear in one of his early poems :

A timid grace sits trembling in her eye,
As loth to meet the rudeness of men's sight,
Yet shedding a delicious lunar light,
That steeps in kind oblivious ecstasy
The care-crazed mind, like some still melody :
Speaking most plain the thoughts which do possess
Her gentle sprite ; peace, and meek quietness,
And innocent loves, and maiden purity.

CHAPTER XVIII

HEARTY, HOMELY, LOVING HERTFORDSHIRE

LAMB'S love of London, which centred in the Temple and Fleet Street, is well known, yet, as his friend Barry Cornwall tells us, " he could feel unaffectedly the simplicity and beauty of a country life. The heartiness of country people went to his heart direct, and remained there for ever. The Fields and the Gladmans, with their homely dwellings and hospitality, drew him to them like magnets."

" The oldest thing I remember," writes Lamb in an Essay of Elia, " is Mackery End . . . a farm-house, delightfully situated within a gentle walk from Wheathampstead. I can just remember having been there on a visit to a great-aunt when I was a child, under the care of Bridget ; who, as I have said, is older than myself by some ten years. . . .

" The house was at that time in the occupation of a substantial yeoman who had married my grandmother's sister. His name was Gladman. My grand-

mother was a Bruton married to a Field. The
Gladmans and the Brutons are still flourishing in
that part of the county, but the Fields are almost
extinct.   More than forty years had elapsed since the
visit I speak of ; and for the greater portion of that
period we had lost sight of the other two branches
also.   Who or what sort of persons inherited Mackery
End—kindred or strange folk—we were afraid almost
to conjecture, but determined some day to explore."

At last the expedition took place and it was in the
heart of June.   " By somewhat a circuitous route,"
continues Lamb, " taking the noble park at Luton in
our way from St. Albans, we arrived at the spot of
our anxious curiosity about noon.   The sight of the
old farm-house, though every trace of it was effaced
from my recollection, affected me with a pleasure
which I had not experienced for many a year.   For
though I had forgotten it we had never forgotten
being there together, and we had been talking about
Mackery End all our lives till memory on my part
became mocked with a phantom of itself. (But)
Bridget's was more a waking bliss than mine, for she
easily remembered her old acquaintance again—some
altered features of course a little grudged at.   At
first indeed she was ready to disbelieve for joy ; but
the scene soon reconstructed itself in her affections—
and she traversed every outpost of the old mansion to
the wood-house, the orchard, the place where the

pigeon-house had stood (house and birds were alike flown) with a breathless impatience of recognition which was more pardonable perhaps than decorous at the age of fifty odd. But Bridget in some things is behind her years.

" The only thing left was to get into the house— and that was a difficulty which to me singly would have been insurmountable ; for I am terribly shy in making myself known to strangers and out-of-date kinsfolk. Love, stronger than scruple, winged my cousin in without me ; but she soon returned with a creature that might have sat to a sculptor for the image of Welcome. It was the youngest of the Glad- mans ; who by marriage with a Bruton had become mistress of the old mansion. A comely brood are the Brutons. Six of them, females, were noted as the handsomest young women in the county. But this adopted Bruton, in my mind was better than they all— more comely. She was born too late to have remem- bered me. She just recollected in early life to have had her cousin Bridget once pointed out to her climb- ing a stile. But the name of kindred and of cousin- ship was enough. Those slender ties that prove slight as gossamer in the rending atmosphere of a metropolis, bind faster, as we found it in hearty, homely, loving Hertfordshire. In five minutes we were thoroughly acquainted as if we had been born and bred up together ; were familiar even to the

calling of each other by our Christian names. To
have seen Bridget and her—it was like the meeting of
the two Scriptural cousins. There was a grace and
dignity, an amplitude of form and stature answering
to her mind, in this farmer's wife, which would have
shined in a palace—or so we thought it. We were
made welcome by husband and wife equally—we and
our friend that was with us—I had almost forgotten
him—but B. F. (Barron Field) will not so soon forget
that meeting, if peradventure he shall read this on the
far-distant shores where the kangaroo haunts."

Here we would pause for a moment to inform the
reader that we also have visited Mackery End and
have seen all that Lamb has so well described. We
too obtained admission to the interior of the old
farm-house, and sat in the best parlour with its
dark panelled walls and its windows of small panes
of glass over-looking the farmyard and also a pretty
flower-garden hard by. Our guide—a servant of
the owners of the place—pointed out to us the various
changes of modern time, but told us that the older
part of the building remains unaltered. So as we
gazed upon the parlour and then proceeded to the
old-world kitchen beyond it we knew that all was
suggestive of the days when Charles Lamb was a
child there.

To return to his account of the hospitable welcome
that he and his sister received from their cousin :

" The fatted calf was made ready," he writes, " or rather was already so, as if in anticipation of our coming, and after an appropriate glass of native wine, never let me forget with what honest pride this hospitable cousin made us proceed to Wheathampstead to introduce us (as some new-found rarity) to her mother and sister Gladmans, who indeed knew something more of us, at a time when she almost knew nothing. With what corresponding kindness we were received by them also—how Bridget's memory, exalted by the occasion, warmed into a thousand half-obliterated recollections of things and persons, to my utter astonishment and her own—and to the astoundment of B. F. who sat by, almost the only thing that was not a cousin there,—old effaced images of more than half-forgotten names and circumstances still crowding back upon her, as words written in lemon come out upon exposure to a friendly warmth—when I forget all this, then may my country cousins forget me ; and Bridget no more remember that in the days of weakling infancy I was her tender charge—as I have been her care in foolish manhood since—in those pretty pastoral walks, long ago, about Mackery End in Hertfordshire."

It must have been about the year 1814–15 that Talfourd first met Lamb, and curiously enough on that same occasion they fell into an intimate talk on serious subjects. After describing his face minutely

—a description we have already given elsewhere—
Talfourd goes on to say: "Who shall describe his
countenance—catch its quivering sweetness—and
fix it for ever in words? . . . Deep thought striving
with humour, the lines of suffering wreathed into
cordial mirth; and a smile of painful sweetness
presents an image to the mind it can as little describe
as forget. He took my arm," continues Talfourd,
"and we walked to the Temple, Lamb stammering
out fine remarks as we walked, and when we reached
his staircase, he detained me with an urgency which
would not be denied, and we mounted to the top story
where an old petted servant called Becky was ready
to receive us. We were soon seated beside a cheerful
fire, hot water and its better adjuncts were before us,
and Lamb insisted on my sitting with him while he
smoked 'one pipe.' . . . I can never forget the
conversation; though the first it was more solemn and
in higher mood than any I ever after had with Lamb
through the whole of our friendship. How it took
such a turn between two strangers, one of them a
lad of not quite twenty, I cannot tell, but so it
happened. We discoursed then of life and death and
our anticipation of a world beyond the grave. Lamb
spoke of these awful themes with the simplest piety,
but expressed his own fond cleavings to life—to all
well-known accustomed things and a shivering (not
shuddering) sense of that which is to come."

" I am in love," he writes, " with this green earth, the face of town and country, the unspeakable rural solitudes, and the sweet security of streets. I would set up my tabernacle here."

We read in his fine Essay, " New Year's Eve ": " Of all sounds of all bells—(bells the music nighest bordering upon heaven)—most solemn and touching is the peal which rings out the Old Year. I never hear it without a gathering up of my mind to a concentration of all the images that have been diffused over the past twelve months ; all I have done or suffered, performed or neglected—in that regretted time. I begin to know its worth as when a person dies. . . . I am none of those who ' Welcome the coming, speed the parting guest.'

" I am naturally, beforehand, shy of novelties ; new books, new faces, new years—from some mental twist, which makes it difficult in me to face the prospective. . . . I plunge into foregone visions and conclusions. . . . I am armour-proof against old discouragements. I forgive or overcome in fancy old adversaries. I play over again for love, as the gamesters phrase it, games for which I once paid so dear. I would scarce now have any of those untoward accidents and events of my life reversed. Methinks, it is better that I should have pined away seven of my goldenest years when I was thrall to the fair hair and fairer eyes of Alice

W——n than that so passionate a love adventure should be lost.

" . . . If I know ought of myself, no one whose mind is retrospective—and mine is painfully so—can have a less respect for his present identity than I have for the man Elia . . . a stammering buffoon ; what you will ; lay it on and spare not ; I subscribe to it all, and much more than thou canst be willing to lay at his door ; but for the child Elia—that ' other me ' there in the background—I must take leave to cherish the remembrance of that young master with as little reference to his stupid changeling of five-and-forty as if it had been a child of some other house and not of my parents. I can cry over its patient small-pox at five and rougher medicaments. I can lay its poor fevered head upon the sick pillow at Christ's and wake with it in surprise at the gentle posture of maternal tenderness hanging over it, that unknown had watched its sleep."

Here we would give a touching poem of Lamb's that seems to be little known, called *A Birthday Thought*. It appears in a volume entitled *Mary and Charles Lamb*, by William Carew Hazlitt (Hazlitt's only son), that was published in 1874.

A BIRTHDAY THOUGHT

Can I, all gracious Providence,
  Can I deserve Thy care ?
Ah, no ! I've not the least pretence
  To bounties which I share.

Have I not been defended still
  From dangers and from death ;
Been safe preserved from every ill
  E'er since Thou gav'st me breath ?

I live once more to see the day
  That brought me first to light ;
Oh, teach my willing heart the way
  To take Thy mercies right.

Tho' dazzling splendour, pomp, and show
  My fortune has denied ;
Yet more than grandeur can bestow
  Content hath well supplied.

I envy no man's birth or fame,
  Their titles, train, or dress ;
Nor has my pride e'er stretched its aim
  Beyond what I possess.

I ask and wish not to appear
  More beauteous, rich, or gay :
Lord, make me wiser every year,
  And better every day.

CHAPTER XIX

FAREWELL TO ESSAY WRITING

TALFOURD tells us that Hazlitt delivered three courses of lectures at the Surrey Institution on " The English Poets," on " The English Comic Writers," and on " The Age of Elizabeth," " which Lamb (under protest against lectures in general) regularly attended, an earnest admirer, amidst crowds with whom the lecturer had ' an imperfect sympathy.' They consisted chiefly of Dissenters who agreed with him in his hatred of Lord Castlereagh, and his love of religious freedom, but who ' loved no plays ' ; of Quakers who approved him as the earnest opponent of slavery and capital punishment but who ' heard no music ' ; of citizens devoted to the new scheme, ' who had a hankering after the improvement of the mind ' ; but to whom his favourite doctrine of its natural disinterestedness was a riddle ; of a few enemies who came to sneer ; and a few friends who were eager to learn and to admire. . . . He startled many of them by observing that since Jacob's dream ' the heavens have gone farther off and become astronomical ' ; a fine extravagance which the ladies and gentlemen who had grown astronomical themselves under the preceding lecturer felt called on to resent as an attack on their severer studies. When he read a well-known extract from Cowper comparing a poor cottager with Voltaire, and had pronounced the line, ' A truth the brilliant Frenchman never knew,' they broke into a joyous shout of self-gratulation, that they were so much wiser than the scornful Frenchman. When he passed by Mrs. Hannah More with observing that ' she had written a great deal which he had never read,' a voice gave expression to the general commiseration and surprise, by calling out, ' More pity for you ! ' They were confounded at his reading, with more emphasis perhaps than discretion, Gay's epigrammatic lines on Sir Richard Blackstone, in which Scriptural persons are too freely hitched into rhyme ; but he went doggedly on to the end, and by his perseverance baffled those who, if he had acknowledged himself wrong by stopping, would have visited with an outburst of displeasure which he felt to be gathering. He once had a more edifying advantage over them. He was enumerating the humanities which endeared Dr. Johnson to his mind, and at the close of an agreeable catalogue, mentioned, as last and noblest, ' his carrying the poor victim of disease and dissipation on his back, through Fleet Street,' at which a titter arose from some, who were struck by the picture as ludicrous, and a murmur from others who deemed the allusion unfit for ears polite ; he paused for an instant, and then added, in his sturdiest and most impressive manner—' an act which realizes the parable of the Good Samaritan,' at which his moral and his delicate hearers shrank rebuked into deep silence."

Talfourd tells us that " Hazlitt had little inclination to talk or write about contemporary authors, and still less to read them. He was with difficulty persuaded to look into the Scotch novels, but when he did so he found them old in substance, though new in form, read them with as much avidity as the rest of the world, and expressed better than anyone else what all the world felt about them.

" Coleridge and Wordsworth were not moderns to him, for they were the inspirers of his youth which was his own antiquity, and the feelings which were the germ of their poetry had sunk deep into his heart. With the exception of the works of these and of his friends Barry Cornwall and Sheridan Knowles, in whose successes he rejoiced, he held modern literature in slight esteem. . . . His ' large discourse of reason ' looked not before but after. He felt it a sacred duty, as a lover of genius and art, to defend the fame of the mighty dead. When the old

painters were assailed in *The Catalogue Raisonné*
of the ' British Institution ' he was ' touched with
noble anger.' All his own vain longings after the
immortality of the works which were libelled—all
the tranquillity and beauty they had shed into his
soul—all his comprehension of the sympathy and
delight of thousands, which, accumulating through
long time, had attested their worth—were fused
together to dazzle and subdue the daring critic who
would disturb the judgment of ages."

We should like to give some passages here from
Hazlitt's beautiful Essay " On a Sun-Dial." The
Sun-Dial in question was near to Venice and it bore
the following motto in Latin : " I count only the
hours that are serene." " What a bland and care-
dispelling feeling ! How the shadows seem to fade
on the dial-plate as the sky lowers and time presents
only a blank unless its progress is marked by
what is joyous, and all that is not happy sinks into
oblivion ! What a fine lesson is conveyed to the
mind—to take no note of time but by its benefits,
to watch only for the smiles and neglect the frowns
of fate ! . . . How different from the common art
of self-tormenting !

" A great advantage which clocks have over
watches and other dumb reckoners of time is that
for the most part they strike the hour—that they are,
as it were, the mouth-pieces of time ; that they not

only point it to the eye, but impress it on the ear, that they 'lend it both an understanding and a tongue.' Time thus speaks to us in an audible and warning voice."

Then turning to his own personal experiences, Hazlitt adds : " When I am in a town, I can hear the clock ; and when I am in the country I can listen to the silence. What I like best is to lie whole mornings on a sunny bank on Salisbury Plain without any object before me, neither knowing nor caring how time passes, and thus ' with light winged toys of feathered idleness ' to melt down hours to moments. Perhaps some such thoughts as I have here set down float before me like motes before my half-shut eyes, or some vivid image of the past by forcible contrast rushes by me—' Diana and her fawn and all the glories of the antique world '—then I start away to prevent the iron from entering my soul and let fall some tears into that stream of time which separates me farther and farther from all I once loved."

He alludes here to the happy days when he was studying to be a painter and visited Paris and the Louvre. " There," he tells us, " I marched delighted through a quarter of a mile of the proudest efforts of the mind of man ; a whole creation of genius, a universe of art."

Now we would turn to Hazlitt's graceful Essay entitled " The Letter-Bell."

" Complaints are frequently made," he writes, " of the vanity and shortness of human life, when if we examine its smallest details they present a world by themselves. The most trifling objects retraced with the eye of memory assume the vividness, the delicacy, and importance of insects seen through a magnifying glass. There is no end of the brilliancy or the variety. . . . As I write this the Letter-Bell passes ; it has a lively pleasant sound with it and not only fills the street with its importunate clamour but rings clear through the length of many half-forgotten years. It strikes upon the ear, it vibrates to the brain, it wakes me from the dream of time, it flings me back upon my first entrance into life, the period of my first coming up to town, when all around was strange, uncertain, adverse, a hubbub of confused noises, a chaos of shifting objects—and when this sound alone startling me with the recollection of a letter I had to send to the friends, brought me, as it were, to myself, made me feel that I had links still connecting me with the universe, and gave me hope and perseverance to persevere. At that loud-tinkling, interrupted sound, the long line of blue hills near the place where I was brought up, waves in the horizon, a golden sunset hovers over them, the dwarf oaks rustle their red leaves in the evening breeze, and the road from Wem to Shrewsbury, by which I first set out on my journey through life, stares me in the face as plain, but from time and change not less visionary and mysterious than the pictures in the *Pilgrim's Progress*. Or if the Letter-Bell does not lead me a dance into the country, it fixes me in the thick of my town recollections I know not how long, long ago. It was a kind of alarm to break off my work when there happened to be company to dinner or when I was going to the play. *That* was going to the play indeed when I went twice a year and had not been more than half a dozen times in my life. Even the idea that anyone else in the house was going was a sort of reflected enjoyment, and conjured up a lively anticipation of the scene. I remember a Miss D——, a maiden lady from Wales (who in her youth was to have been married to an earl), tantalized me greatly in this way by talking all day of going to see Mrs. Siddons's ' airs and graces ' at night in some favourite part ; and when the Letter-Bell announced that the time was approaching, and its last receding sound lingered in the ear, or was lost in silence, how anxious and uneasy I became lest she and her company should not be in time to get good places—lest the curtain should draw up before they arrived—and lest I should lose one line or look in the intelligent report which I should hear the next morning !

" . . . How often have I put off writing a letter till it was too late ! How often have I had to run after the postman with it—now missing, now recovering, the sound of his bell—breathless, angry with myself—then hearing the welcome sound come full round a corner—and seeing the scarlet costume which set all my fear and self-reproaches at rest ! . . . At times I have sat and watched the decaying embers in a little back painting-room (just as the wintry day declined), and brooded over the half-finished copy of a Rembrandt, or a landscape by Vangoyen, placing it where it might catch a dim gleam of the light from the fire ; while the Letter-Bell was the only sound that drew my thoughts to the world without, and reminded me that I had a task to perform in it. As to that landscape, methinks I see it now.

> The slow canal, the yellow-blossomed vale,
> The willow-tufted bank, the gliding sail.

" There was a windmill, too, with a poor, low, clay-built cottage beside it. How delighted I was when I had made the tremulous, undulating reflection in the water, and saw the dull canvas become a lucid mirror of the commonest features of nature ! "

In the year 1828 Hazlitt's short and gifted life was nearing its end, and he wrote his touching Essay entitled " Farewell to Essay Writing." In it his love of nature and all that is beautiful shines forth, and solaces him for many a trial caused by failing health. He was then staying at his cottage in Winterslow.

Referring to the pleasures of Society, he says : " Instead of these give me the robin redbreast, pecking the crumbs at the door or warbling on the leafless spray ; the same glancing form that has followed me wherever I have been and ' done its spiriting gently ' ; in the rich notes of the thrush that startle the ear of winter, and seem to have drunk up the full draught of joy from the very sense of contrast. To these I adhere and am faithful, for they are true to me and . . . are dear in themselves, and dearer for the sake of what is departed, leading me back (by the hand) to that dreaming world in the innocence of which they sat and made sweet music, waking the promises of future years and answered by the eager throbbings of my own breast. . . .

" Not far from the spot where I write, I first read Chaucer's *Flower and Leaf*, and was charmed with that young beauty, shrouded in her bower, and listening with ever fresh delight to the repeated song of the nightingale close by her—the impression of the scene, the vernal landscape, the cool of the morning, the gushing notes of the songstress is as vivid as if it had been of yesterday. . . . I used to walk out at this time with Mr. and Miss Lamb of an evening to look at the Claude Lorraine skies over our heads melting from azure into purple and gold, and to gather mushrooms that sprung up at our feet to throw into our hashed mutton at supper."

We have an interesting glimpse of Hazlitt at about this same period when he was in town, from the pen of Charles Cowden Clarke.* " It was our good fortune," he writes, " to see a magnificent copy that Hazlitt made of Titian's portrait of Hippolito dei Medici when we called at his lodgings one evening. The painting, a mere stretched canvas without frame, was standing on an old-fashioned couch in one corner of the room leaning against the wall, and we remained opposite to it for some time, while Hazlitt stood by holding the candle high up so as to throw the light well on to the picture, descanting enthusiastically on the merits of the original. The beam from the candle falling on his own finely intellectual head with its iron-grey hair, its square potential forehead, its massive mouth and chin and eyes full of earnest fire, formed a glorious picture in itself and remains a luminous vision for ever upon our memory. . . . Under that straightforward, hard-hitting, direct-telling manner of his, both in writing and speaking, Hazlitt had a depth of gentleness—even tenderness—of feeling on certain subjects ; manly friendship, womanly sympathy, touched him to the core, and any token of either would bring a sudden expression into his eyes very beautiful as well as very heart-stirring to look upon. We have seen this expression more than once, and can recall its appealing charm,

* See his *Recollections of Writers*, published in 1878.

its wonderful irradiation of the strong features and squarely-cut rugged under portion of the face."

Hazlitt's power of brain work continued unimpaired to the end of his life. He had been working for some time past at his *Life of Napoleon*, and was able to complete it shortly before his death. Some critics have maintained that it is principally by this work that his fame will last. We do not share that opinion. Surely his Essays, so full as they are of beauty of thought, of knowledge and keen appreciation of art ; all given to us in his own special phraseology which in its way stands quite alone, must rank first. In one of his later Essays he says : " I have the same favourite books, pictures, passages that I ever had : I may therefore presume that they will last me my life—nay, I may indulge a hope that my thoughts will survive me." This they have assuredly done. The wide popularity of the Essays is proved by the endless new editions of them which are constantly appearing before the public—and they have probably done more to mould the better style of modern literary work than can be calculated.

Hazlitt died on September 18, 1830, at the age of fifty-two only. He had suffered for long past from an organic disease which must account for any irritability of temper that he was sometimes accused of. His last illness was in 8, Frith Street, Soho, and happily his old friends Charles and Mary

Lamb were at that time lodging close at hand. Charles was with him when he died as well as his much-loved son William. His last words recorded by the latter were, " I have had a happy life."

He was laid to rest in the burying-ground of St. Anne's, Soho, where, in spite of its being in the heart of London, there are trees to be seen even now waving their branches in the breeze beneath a blue sky, such as Hazlitt loved to look upon.

CHAPTER XX

A WEDDING

WHEN the Scotch novels began to appear Hazlitt, we have seen, strove against succumbing to the general fever in favour of them, but when he had given in he read them " with avidity " and enjoyed them to the full. But Lamb, on the contrary, was too completely wedded to the old books of the seventeenth and early eighteenth century to be able to turn from them lightly to a new writer, however able he might appear to be. But " the good-naturedness of Sir Walter to all his contemporaries won his admiration," as Talfourd tells us, " and he heartily rejoiced in the greatness of his fame and the rich rewards showered upon him, and desired that they might accumulate for the ' glory of literature and the triumph of kindness.' He used to speak with gratitude and pleasure of the circumstances under which he saw him once in Fleet Street. A man, in the dress of a mechanic, stopped him just at Inner

Temple Gate and, touching his hat, said : ' I beg your pardon, sir, but perhaps you would like to see Sir Walter Scott, that is he just crossing the road,' and Lamb stammered out his hearty thanks to his truly humane informer."

It seems that on one occasion Charles Lamb had written to Sir Walter about Godwin's financial difficulties, and had at once received from him a sum of ten pounds to be given to Godwin anonymously. In Lamb's letter of thanks he alludes to an invitation he had received to visit Sir Walter in Scotland.

" I cannot pass over your kind expressions to myself," he writes. " It is not likely that I shall ever find myself in Scotland, but should the event ever happen, I should be proud to pay my respects to you in your own land. My disparagement of heaths and highlands—if I said any such thing in half earnest— you must put down as a piece of the old Vulpine policy. I must make the most of the spot I am chained to and console myself for my flat destiny as well as I am able. I know very well our mole-hills are not mountains, but I must cocker them up and make them look as big and as handsome as I can that we may both be satisfied." *

The reader will remember often meeting with Admiral Burney and Mrs. Burney (the original of " Mrs. Battle upon Whist ") in the earlier chapters

* See *Life of Charles Lamb,* by E. V. Lucas.

of this work, as forming a part of the " Good Company in Old Westminster." They may also remember their son Martin, a valued friend of Lamb's, and their daughter Sally. The latter was much at the Rickmans' house and is described by Mrs. Lefroy in the *Recollections*. After mentioning the old musical Doctor, the father of the Admiral, she says, "there was naturally a very Burney respect for music in the family and Sally learnt Thorough Bass and played classic music in a very professional manner."

In the month of April 1821, Sally was married to her cousin John Payne. The wedding must have taken place from No. 26, James Street, Westminster, where the Burneys were then living. Lamb, who was present on the occasion, made it the subject of one of the Essays of Elia entitled " The Wedding," a portion of which we will give here. Canon Ainger, in his " Notes " upon this Essay, points out that some of the circumstances in it are not strictly correct, but " it was upon them," he remarks, " that he built up this idyllic little story." It was a plan that he frequently followed in his Essays. They do not pretend to be absolutely biographical, but admit of Lamb's giving vent at will to his own sweet fancies. The names are usually altered, and in this case the reader must substitute, in his own mind, " Sally " for " Emily."

" I do not know when I have been better pleased,"

writes Elia, " than at being invited last week to be present at the wedding of a friend's daughter. I like to make one at these ceremonies, which to us old people give back our youth in a manner and restore our gayest season in the remembrance of our own success, or the regrets, scarcely less tender, of our own youthful disappointments. . . . On these occasions I am sure to be in good humour for a week or two after, and enjoy a reflected honeymoon. Being without a family I am flattered with these temporary adoptions into a friend's family ; I feel a sort of cousinhood or uncleship for the season ; I am inducted into degrees of affinity ; and, in the participated socialities of the little community, I lay down for a brief while my solitary bachelorship. . . .

" The union itself had been long settled, but its celebration had been hitherto deferred, to an almost unreasonable state of suspense in the lovers, by some invincible prejudice which the bride's father had unhappily contracted upon the subject of the too early marriages of females. . . . We all began to be afraid that a suit which as yet had abated none of its ardours, might at last be lingered on till passion had time to cool and love go out in the experiment. But a little wheedling on the part of his wife, who was by no means a party to these overstrained notions, joined to some serious expostulations on the part of his friends, who from the growing infirmities of the old gentleman could not promise ourselves many years' enjoyment of his company, and were anxious to bring matters to a conclusion, during his lifetime, at length prevailed ; and on Monday last the daughter of my old friend Admiral ———, having attained the *womanly* age of nineteen, was conducted to the church by her pleasant cousin J—— who told some few years older. . . .

" It had been fixed that the ceremony should be gone through at an early hour, to give time for a little *déjeuné* afterwards to which a select party of friends had been invited. We were in church a little before the clock struck eight.

" Nothing could be more judicious or graceful than the dress of the bridesmaids—the charming Miss Foresters—on this morning. To give the bride an opportunity of shining singly they had cóme habited all in green. I am ill at describing female apparel ; but while *she* stood at the altar in vestments white and candid as her thoughts, in sacrificial whiteness, they assisted in robes such as might become Diana's nymphs—Foresters indeed—as such who had not yet come to the resolution of putting off cold virginity. (Among the elders there might be some grave looks) but with the young people all was merriment and shaking of hands and congratulations, and kissing away the bride's tears and kissing from her in return.

" My friend the Admiral was in fine wig and buckle

N

on this occasion—a striking contrast to his usual neglect of personal appearance. He did not once shove up his borrowed locks, his custom ever at his morning studies, to betray the few grey stragglers of his own beneath them. He wore an air of thoughtful satisfaction. I trembled for the hour which at length approached, when after a protracted *breakfast* of three hours, if stores of cold fowls, hams, etc., can deserve so meagre an appellation—the coach was announced which was come to carry off the bride and bridegroom for a season, as custom has sensibly ordained, into the country ; upon which design, wishing them a felicitous journey, let us return to the assembled guests.

> As when a well-graced actor leaves the stage,
> The eyes of men
> Are idly bent on him that enters next,

so idly did we bend our eyes upon one another, when the chief performers in the morning's pageant had vanished. None told his tale. None sipped her glass. The poor Admiral made an effort,—it was not much. I had anticipated so far. Even the infinity of full satisfaction that had betrayed itself through the prim looks and quiet deportment of his lady began to wane into something of misgiving. No one knew whether to take their leave or stay. We seemed assembled upon a silly occasion. In this crisis betwixt tarrying and departure, I must do

THE HOUSE OF COMMONS BEFORE 1834

justice to a foolish talent of mine which had otherwise like to have brought me into disgrace in the fore-part of the day ; I mean a power in any emergency of thinking and giving vent to all manner of strange nonsense. In this awkward dilemma I found it sovereign. I rattled off some of my most excellent absurdities. All were willing to be relieved at any expense of reason from the pressure of the intolerable vacuum which had succeeded to the morning bustle. By this means I was fortunate in keeping together the better part of the company to a late hour ; and a rubber of whist (the Admiral's favourite game) with some rare strokes of chance as well as skill which came opportunely on his side—lengthened out till midnight—dismissed the old gentleman at last to his bed with comparatively easy spirits.

" I have been at my old friend's various times since. I do not know a visiting place where every guest is so perfectly at his ease ; nowhere where harmony is so strangely the result of confusion. Everybody is at cross-purposes, yet the effect is so much better than uniformity. Contradictory orders, servants pulling one way, master and mistress driving some other, yet both diverse ; visitors huddled up in corners ; chairs unsymmetrized ; candles dispersed by chance ; meals at odd hours, tea and supper at once, or the latter preceding the former ; the host and the guest conferring, yet each upon a different topic, each understanding himself, neither trying to understand nor hear the other ; draughts and politics, chess and political economy, cards and conversation on nautical matters going on at once, without the hope or indeed the wish of distinguishing them, make it altogether the most perfect *concordia discors* you shall meet with.   Yet somehow the old house is not quite what it should be.   The Admiral still enjoys his pipe, but there is no Emily to fill it for him.   The instrument stands where it stood, but she is gone whose delicate touch could sometimes for a short minute appease the warring elements.   He has learnt, as Marvel expresses it, to make his destiny his choice.   He bears bravely up, but he does not come out with his flashes of wild wit so thick as formerly.   His sea-songs seldom escape him.   His wife too looks as if she wanted some younger body to scold and set to rights.   We all miss a junior presence. It is wonderful how one young maiden freshens up and keeps green the paternal roof.   Old and young seem to have an interest in her so long as she is not absolutely disposed of.   The youthfulness of the house is flown.   Emily is married."

CHAPTER XXI

A MOMENTOUS INTERVIEW

L AMB was fond of visiting the Universities in vacation time, and frequently spent his summer holiday month in one of them. " To such a one as myself," he writes in " Oxford in the Vacation," " who has been defrauded in his young years of the sweet food of an academic Institution, nowhere is so pleasant to while away a few idle weeks as at one or other of the Universities. Their vacation too at this time of the year falls in so pat with ours. Here I can take my walks unmolested and fancy myself of what degree or standing I please. . . . I can rise at the Chapel-bell and dream that it rings for me. . . . When the peacock vein rises I strut a Gentleman Commoner. In graver moments I proceed Master of Arts. Indeed, I do not think I am much unlike that respectable character. I have seen your dim-eyed vergers, and bed-makers in spectacles, drop a bow or a curtsey as I pass, wisely mistaking me for something of the sort. . . . I go about in black which favours the notion. . . .

" The walks at these times are so much one's own—the tall trees of Christ's, the groves of Magdalen! The halls deserted and with open doors inviting one to slip in unperceived, and pay a devoir to some Founder or noble or royal Benefactress (that should have been ours) whose portrait seems to smile upon their overlooked beadsman and to adopt me for their own."

In the month of August 1815, Mary Lamb paid her first visit to Cambridge in company with her brother.

She writes to a friend on the occasion : " In my life I never spent so many pleasant hours together as I did at Cambridge. We were walking the whole time—out of one college into another. I liked them all best. The little gloomy ones because they were little gloomy ones. I felt as if I could live and die in them and never wish to speak again. And the fine grand Trinity College. Oh, how fine it was ! And King's College Chapel, what a place ! I heard the Cathedral service there, and having been no great church goer of late years, that and the painted windows and the general effect of the whole thing affected me wonderfully.

" I certainly like St. John's College best. I had seen least of it having only been over it once, so on the morning we returned, I got up at six o'clock and wandered into it by myself—by myself indeed, for there was nothing alive to be seen, but one cat who followed me about like a dog. Then I went over Trinity, but nothing hailed me there, not even a cat.

" On the Sunday we met with a pleasant thing. We had been congratulating each other that we had come alone to enjoy, as the miser his feast, all our sights greedily to ourselves, but having seen all, we began to grow flat and wish for this and t'other body with us, when we were accosted by a young gownsman whose face we knew, but where or how we had seen him we could not tell and were obliged to ask him his name. He proved to be a young man we had seen twice at Alsager's. He turned out a very pleasant fellow—showed us the insides of places—we took him to our Inn to dinner and we drank tea with him in such a delicious College room and then again he supped with us. We made our meals as short as possible, to lose no time, and walked our young conductor almost off his legs. Even when the fried eels were ready for supper and coming up, having a message from a man who we had bribed for the purpose that we might see Oliver Cromwell, who was not at home when we called to see him, we sallied out again and made him a visit by candlelight—and so ended our sights. . . .

" Returning home down Old Fetter Lane, I could hardly keep from crying to think it was all over. With what pleasure (Charles) showed me Jesus College where Coleridge was (and) the house where Lloyd lived ! " *

It was on one of Charles and Mary Lamb's visits to Cambridge, Talfourd tells us, " that they met with a little girl who, being, in a manner, alone in the world, engaged their sympathy and soon riveted their affections. Emma Isola was the daughter of Mr. Charles Isola, who had been one of the ' esquire bedells ' of the University ; her grandfather, Agastino Isola, had been compelled to fly from Milan because a friend took up an English book in his apartment which he had carelessly left in view. This good old man numbered among his pupils, Gray the poet, Mr. Pitt and (in later days) Wordsworth whom he instructed in the Italian language. His little grand-daughter, at the time when she had the good fortune to win the regard of Mr. Lamb, had lost both her parents, and was spending her holidays with an aunt at the house of Mr. Ayrton. There Lamb generally played his evening rubber during his stay at Cambridge. The liking which both Lamb and his sister took for the little orphan led to their begging her of her aunt for the next holidays ; their regard for her increased ; she regularly spent the holidays with them

* See *Charles Lamb*, by E. V. Lucas.

till she left school and afterwards was adopted as a daughter." This circumstance brought much happiness into the Lamb household. " Lamb was fond of taking long walks in the country," and as Miss Lamb's strength was not always equal to these pedestrian excursions, Emma became his constant companion in walks which even extended " to the green fields of pleasant Hertfordshire." And Mary, " who had a most tender sympathy with the young," much enjoyed the daily intercourse with her little companion. She was also well qualified to assist her in her studies, for had she not recently given lessons to both young William Hazlitt and Victoria Novello (afterwards Mrs. Charles Cowden Clarke) in the rudiments of the Latin language, emphasizing the grand verse-music of its poetry and inspiring them to love and admire that which she herself had learnt to love and admire ?

Lamb had long felt the burden of his work at the India House becoming more and more irksome, and he writes in an Essay of Elia (in which he changes the real name of the streets) :

" It is now six-and-thirty years since I took my seat at the desk in Mincing Lane. Melancholy was the transition at fourteen from the abundant playtime and the frequently intervening vacations of school-days to the eight, nine and sometimes ten-hours-a-day attendance at the Counting-house. But time partially reconciles us to anything. I gradually became content—doggedly contented as wild animals in cages.

" It is true I had my Sundays to myself . . . and besides Sundays I had a day at Easter and a day at Christmas, with a full week in the summer to go and air myself in my native fields of Hertfordshire. This last was a great indulgence ; and the prospect of its recurrence, I believe, alone kept me up through the year and made my durance tolerable. (Even) the prospect of its coming threw something of an illumination upon the darker side of my captivity. Without it, as I have said, I could scarcely have sustained my thraldom."

But Lamb could write playfully even of his heaviest trials, and in a letter of congratulation to his friend Procter (Barry Cornwall) upon his marriage he remarks : " I am married myself—to a severe step-wife who keeps me not at bed and board but at desk and board and is jealous of my morning aberration. I cannot slip out and congratulate kinder unions. It is well she leaves me alone o' nights. The d——d Day-hag *Business*. She is even now peeping over me to see I am writing no Love Letters. I come, my dear. Where is the Indigo Sale Book ? Twenty adieus, my dear friend, till we meet."

By the beginning of the year 1825 Lamb, whose strength was much affected by his long desk work, determined, in spite of anxiety for the future, to express his willingness to the Directors of the India House to resign his post.

He has described the whole affair graphically in an Essay of Elia entitled " The Superannuated Man," which he wrote immediately after the occurrence had taken place. The only change he has made in the Essay is in transforming the Directors of the India House into a private Firm of Merchants.

After sending in his letter to the Directors he began to feel misgivings on the subject and to fear that he might have acted unwisely.

" A week passed in this manner," writes Elia, " the most anxious one, I verily believe, in my life, when on the evening of the 12th April, just as I was quitting my desk to go home (it might be about eight o'clock), I received an awful summons to attend the presence of the whole assembled firm in the formidable back parlour. I thought, Now my time has surely come, I have done for myself, I am going to be told that they have no longer occasion for me. L——— I could see, smiled at the terror I was in, which was a little relief to me, when, to my utter astonishment, B———, the eldest partner, began a formal harangue to me on the length of my services, my very meritorious conduct during the whole of the time (the deuce, thought I, how did he find out that ? I protest I never had the confidence to think as much). He

went on to descant on the expediency of retiring at a
certain time of life (how my heart panted !) and,
asking me a few questions as to the amount of my own
property, of which I have a little, ended with a
proposal, to which his three partners nodded a grave
assent, that I should accept from the house, which
I had served so well, a pension for life to the amount
of two-thirds of my accustomed salary.   A magnificent offer !   I do not know what I answered between
surprise and gratitude, but it was understood that I
accepted their proposal, and was told that I was free
from that hour to leave the service.   I stammered
out a bow, and at just ten minutes after eight I went
home—forever."

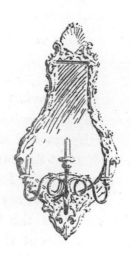

CHAPTER XXII

A LEADER OF THE GOOD COMPANY

ONE of the first uses that Lamb made of his freedom from office work, we are told, was to pay visits in the near country with Mary. In summer-time they were often at Enfield. In a letter to Southey Lamb says: "Mary walks her twelve miles a day some days and I my twenty on others. 'Tis all holiday with me now, you know. The change works admirably."

After a while Lamb made up his mind to quit London and to reside altogether in Enfield. Mary's illnesses had become more frequent and of longer duration and she was no longer equal to managing a household. They therefore made arrangements with " a very comfortable old couple " to board and lodge them. " We use a sort of common table," writes Lamb. " Nevertheless we have reserved a private one for an old friend." Lamb gives a description of the ménage in a letter to Wordsworth. " Our providers," he writes, " are an honest pair. Dame

Westwood and her husband, he, when the light of prosperity shined on them, a modestly thriving haberdasher within Bow Bells, retired since with something under a competence ; writes himself parcel gentleman, hath borne parish offices ; sings fine old sea-songs at threescore-and-ten ; sighs only now and then when he thinks that he has a son on his hands about fifteen whom he finds a difficulty in getting out into the world ; and then checks a sigh with muttering, prettily, not meaning to be heard : ' I have married my daughter, however ' ; takes the weather as it comes ; outsides it to town in severest season ; and o' winter nights tells old stories, not tending to literature (how comfortable to author-rid folks !), and has *one anecdote* upon which and about forty pounds a year he seems to have retired in green old age."

Young Thomas Westwood, the son alluded to, recorded his reminiscences of the Lambs in later years.* He writes : " My first glimpse of the Lambs' household is as vivid in my recollection as if it were of yesterday. It was in Enfield. Leaning idly out of window I saw a group of three issuing from the ' gambogey looking cottage ' close at hand : a slim middle-aged man in quaint uncontemporary habiliments, a rather shapeless bundle of an old lady in a bonnet like a mob-cap, and a young girl, while

* See *Mary Lamb*, by Mrs. Gilchrist.

before them bounded a riotous dog (Hood's immortal Dash) holding a board with ' This house to be Let ' on it in his jaws. Lamb was on his way back to the house-agent, and that was his fashion of announcing that he had taken the premises.

" I soon grew to be on intimate terms with my neighbour," he continues, " who let me loose in his library. My heart yearns even now to those old books. Their faces seem all familiar to me, even their patches and botches, the work of a wizened old cobbler hard by, for little wotted Lamb of Roger Paynes and Charles Lewises. A cobbler was his book-binder ; and the rougher the restoration the greater the success. . . . When any notable visitors made their appearance at the cottage Mary Lamb's benevolent tap at my window-pane seldom failed to summon me out, and I was presently ensconced in a quiet corner of their sitting-room half hid in some great man's shadow."

In the spring of 1833 the Lambs made their last removal from Enfield to Edmonton. Emma Isola had become engaged to be married to their friend Mr. Moxon, the publisher, and her marriage was approaching. Lamb had determined, under the circumstances, to live altogether with his sister " whether in her sanity or madness." The loss of their adopted daughter was felt keenly, though she and her husband did all they could to lessen it. In this same year 1833 the *Last Essays of Elia* appeared before the public, containing some of Lamb's finest writings and proving how clear and vigorous his mind had remained in spite of grievous trials.

One more severe trial came to him in 1833 in the death of Coleridge. " He was my fifty years old friend," writes Lamb, " without a dissension."

When the two friends were quite young men Charles and his sister Mary were visiting Coleridge at Nether-Stowey and enjoying long walks in that beautiful country, but Coleridge could not accompany them owing to a temporary accident to one of his feet. But he used his enforced idleness to compose the pretty poem entitled *This Lime-tree Bower my Prison*, and now, during his last illness, " Thoughts of his youth came to him," he said, " like breezes from the Spice Islands," and he wrote beneath the poem a little while before he died :

" Charles and Mary Lamb. Dear to my heart, yea as it were *my heart*.

" S. T. C. Æ. 63. 1834.

1797
1834
———
37 years."

Lamb was soon to follow him.

" A short time only before Lamb's fatal illness," writes Talfourd, " he yielded to my urgent importunity and met a small party of his friends at dinner at my house, where we had provided for him some of the few articles of food which seemed to hit his fancy . . . with the hope of exciting his very delicate appetite. . . . We were not disappointed ; he ate with a relish not usual with him of late years and passed the evening in his happiest mood.

" Among the four or five friends who met him on this occasion, the last in which I saw him in health, were his old friends Mr. Barron Field, Mr. Procter (Barry Cornwall) and Mr. Forster, author of the *Lives of Eminent English Statesmen*, a friend of comparatively recent date, but one with whom Lamb found himself as much at home as if he had known him for years. Mr. Field, in a short but excellent memoir of Lamb, has brought this evening vividly to recollection. . . . After justly eulogizing Lamb's sense of ' The Virtue of Suppression in Writing,' Mr. Field proceeds : ' We remember at the very last supper we ate with him, he quoted a passage from Prior's *Henry and Emma* which he declared to be a vapid paraphrase of the old poem of *The Nutbrowne Mayde*. After giving several pompous couplets of Prior's poem, he made us mark the modest simplicity with which the noble youth discloses himself to his mistress in the old poem :

O

Now understand
To Westmoreland
Which is my heritage
I will you bring
And with a ring
By way of marriage
I will you take
And lady make
As shortly as I can.
So have you won
An Earle's son
And not a banish'd man.

How he loved these old rhymes!' remarks Field, 'and with what justice!'"

A short time after this happy little gathering had taken place Lamb met with an accident. He was taking his daily morning walk on the London Road as far as the inn where John Gilpin's ride is pictured, when he stumbled against a stone, we are told, fell, and slightly injured his face. The wounds seemed healing when erysipelas in the head came on and he sank beneath the disease, but happily without pain. . . . " His voice gradually grew fainter as he murmured the names of some old friends, and sank into death as placidly as into sleep."

" To him who never gave pain to a human being ; whose genius yielded nothing but instruction and delight," writes Barry Cornwall, " was awarded a calm and easy death. No man, it is my belief," he adds, " was ever loved or lamented more sincerely than Charles Lamb."

It was long before poor Mary Lamb could realize the loss she had sustained, but her mind was sufficiently clear at the time to enable her to point out to their friends the spot in Edmonton Churchyard where her brother had desired to be buried.

There the brother and sister, who were so much to each other in life, now lie side by side.

CHAPTER XXIII

THE GREAT FIRE

OUR narration of the " Good Company in Old Westminster and the Temple " comes to a close with the passing away of its most distinguished members, but we thank God that their works remain with us to raise and inspire the minds of each succeeding generation. This is a noble legacy !

Much had been going on in the political world during our period, of which we have not written, for our leading characters were not politicians but essentially men of Letters. We cannot, however, pass over the great event of 1832 without alluding to the Reform Bill passed that year for which end our forbears toiled without ceasing.

We would close this volume with an account of the great fire of 1834 which demolished the Houses of Parliament of Old Westminster and brought about great changes in the neighbourhood.

We are able to quote the account from Mrs.

THE HOUSE OF LORDS BEFORE 1834

Lefroy's interesting *Recollections* and also from a letter written by her sister, Frances Rickman, on the spot.*

In the month of October 1834, Mrs. Lefroy (Anne Rickman) was staying with an uncle at Hambrook in Sussex, and she writes on the 16th instant : " As he and I were on our way through Chichester to a dinner party, a large letter was thrust into the window of the carriage with ' Immediate ' written in large letters ; this was to tell us that the Houses of Parliament were then in flames ! This letter from Frances was penned by the light of the fire which caused our windows to be too hot to touch, and the air filled with sparks and burning paper."

This letter from Frances Rickman is dated " Palace Yard, 17th Oct., $\frac{1}{2}$ past 3 a.m.," and begins :

" Thank God, my dearest Anne, after near eight hours of dreadful doubt, we seem all safe, though I am still partly lighted by the still blazing House of Commons ! I fear you will hear of the awful fire before this reaches you. . . . I will give you as collected an account as I can, for my legs ache and I could not sleep, so I may as well write. After dinner at $\frac{1}{2}$ past six this evening, Papa and Mamma taking a nap, in came Ellis, ' I think, Miss, there is a small fire broke out at the House of Lords.' I said, ' Come with me to the leads to see it,' and there even

---

* This letter has appeared in the *Life of John Rickman*, by Orlo Williams.

then a volume of flame was blowing towards the Wildes'. Papa at first thought it could be got under, but soon it fearfully grew and we had little doubt the Hall would catch. The House of Lords we could not see, but some heard that it and Mr. Ley's and the Library were destroyed ; then the flames burst from the House of Commons windows and sooner than I could believe the interior of that was destroyed. Now see my view, the west window in bow-room my prospect—front state rooms of Speaker's remain entire (outwardly), red smoke rises from the quadrangle, and the open House of Common's arches (ruined, like Fountains Abbey) are filled with an orange light, nearly the whole of the south end of the Speaker's is destroyed. . . ."

We would pause here for a moment to explain in Mrs. Lefroy's words how the fire originated. " It was the result," she writes, " of a very foolish proceeding. There was an old and cumbrous store of Tallies (wooden staffs a yard long) in the Exchequer next door to us and it was decided that they were useless and should be destroyed . . . and that, as Parliament was not sitting, it would be the opportunity to thrust them into the large fire-place which heated the flues under the House of Lords. . . . You may suppose that very soon the flues became red hot so that the whole floor of the House of Lords is supposed to have burst into flame at once. Our

THE GREAT FIRE OF 1834

private coachman, Robert Bowles, was the person who perceived an ominous smoke and first gave the alarm. The Speaker and family were out of town. Very quickly fire-engines were called, but so intricate were the approaches to the old buildings that it was difficult to reach the fire. . . . The Speaker's Quadrangle and the small space for affording light to the south window of the Hall were the only places where water could be applied externally. . . . The fire had first appeared in the upper floor of the west side of the House of Lords buildings ; and in ten minutes the flame was seen to ascend 10 yards above the roof of the House of Lords. The wind blew from the south which caused it to spread on to the House of Commons and the Hall and our house. Great anxiety was felt for Westminster Hall with its magnificent wooden roof.

" Sir Francis Palgrave saw the fire distinctly from Hampstead and came up to his office in Poet's Corner, by the Chapter House of Westminster Abbey, and he described the scene as he viewed it through the window of Henry 7th Chapel, as most sublime, the old banners hanging over the Knights' seats lighted up. There was also a full moon that night which gave a very mixed effect."

" Papa and Mr. Payne," writes Frances, " took me out to the corner of Palace Yard to see the Abbey, such a grand sight as I pray I may never see again ;

the bright moon in dark clouds, and the clear red and blue and yellow light. Oh! no one who did not see it can picture it! I first ran to the Wildes, who with Mr. Gurtkin were in an agony that, as first appeared probable, they would be burned ; even then blazing papers were floating over and in their garden. I brought some valuables to our house. But soon the tide turned and *we* were in danger, so Papa thought we should put things together. . . . Poor Mamma was much overcome at first but that made me stronger ; as I felt I must look to every thing, Papa being then rather provokingly easy. By this time we had many helps and constant knocking at the door. . . . Presently in came poor Mr. Manning, who had spent the day out. . . . He saw the fire in Oxford Street and rushed down. . . . James the Dean of Ripon's servant sent to help, Mrs. Doctor Holland's coachman and footman here when there came a knock and Henry Taylor answered my ' your name if you please ' before I let him in. He had a tall elegant friend with him, Mr. Edward Villiers, and they insisted on being active chief managers under me, and worked furiously." This same Edward Villiers, in a letter given in the *Life of John Rickman*, writes : " I saw it all, at least from the commencement till one o'clock, and part of the time was very actively engaged. I left the Athenæum, where I had been dining with Taylor and Rickman, and we went to see if Rickman wanted assistance, as his house stands on one side of

Westminster Hall in immediate danger. I assisted in gutting his house, and such a scene of confusion never was seen. I got also a most splendid view of the fire which was burning all around the house. . . . (Then) the lighting up of the Abbey—a more beautiful sight than that never was beheld.

" All the attempts to arrest the fire were for hours unsuccessful; they deserved to be, for they were really contemptible, considering the age in which we live—nothing ready, nothing effective when it was ready and no management whatever."

Frances Rickman continues her account of the hasty removal of their furniture. " H. T. getting coaches, taking their number, filling them and sending a servant on the box of each to unload . . . for the books were tied in sheets, drawers emptied, everything dismantled. . . . Captain Colquhoun was directing in the Speaker's House. They knocked in the roof. The furniture all thrown out of the windows, even china, mirrors &c. . . . The Police order was, however, beautiful. The Horse Guards down and H. T. as he came met Lord Munster and considerately asked him for a dozen soldiers to stand at our door. What a subject for his next poem !

" I am truly thankful that I was able to use more energy than I can now believe possible. Truly strength is given in the day of trial."

" At 9 o'clock," we are told, " the fire was in contact with Westminster Hall which till 12 o'clock was in much danger, the flames surrounding its South end and occasionally penetrating into it from the east through the boarded window of connection with the adjoining Speaker's Gallery. The Speaker's Quadrangle and the small space for affording light to the south window of the Hall were the only places where water could be applied externally.

"The flames then advanced along the east side of the Speaker's Quadrangle, when the wind ceased and at one o'clock became northerly. Also the tide rose, and a floating Fire-engine was enabled to throw water on the House with great force."

"I hope the Tapestry is saved," writes Frances. "Fancy the Spanish Armada and all destroyed!"

But later she writes : "Half-past 6 Daylight and after a hard fight to save the Hall, the fire is all out."

INDEX

BY THE SAME AUTHOR

MARIA EDGEWORTH AND HER CIRCLE

IN THE DAYS OF BONAPARTE AND BOURBON.

With numerous illustrations by ELLEN G. HILL. Demy
8vo, 21s. net.

Morning Post.—"The accomplished authoress of *The House in St. Martin's Street*, of *Juniper Hall*, and of a remarkable volume on Jane Austen, has now given to the reading world a very animated portrait of Maria Edgeworth, in the middle years of her long life, when she was already famous and about to make the acquaintance of Sir Walter Scott. . . . Endlessly interesting are the letters contained in Miss Hill's book."

Spectator.—". . . A lively and very readable book. . . . It has amusing stories of English as well as French society. Various quaint literary figures of the times are agreeably presented : in fact, there is scarcely a famous name in France or England with whom the brilliant Irish writer has not some acquaintance or connection, and the effect of the whole book is that of a series of pleasant social pictures taken from the first twenty years of the nineteenth century."

JANE AUSTEN : HER HOMES AND HER

FRIENDS. With numerous illustrations by ELLEN G.
HILL, and Reproductions from Old Portraits. New
Edition. Crown 8vo, 6s. net.

MARY RUSSELL MITFORD
AND
HER SURROUNDINGS

With numerous Illustrations by ELLEN G. HILL.

Demy 8vo, 21s. net.

Morning Post.—" A biography that in itself has many of the charms distinguishing its famous subject."

The British Weekly.—"The author and the artist have been unsparing in their careful research, and they have a sunny faculty of admiration and sympathy which sets their subjects in their right places with all their charms and graces. This volume has been prepared with a most loving care."

JOHN LANE THE BODLEY HEAD LTD., VIGO ST., W.1